A GUIDE TO AMERICAN FOOTBALL

A GUIDE TO

AMERICAN FOOTBALL

KEN THOMAS

STANLEY PAUL
London

In association with
Channel Four Television

This edition published by Stanley Paul Limited 1993

1 3 5 7 9 10 8 6 4 2

© Ken Thomas 1983, 1984, 1985, 1986, 1988, 1989, 1993

The right of Ken Thomas to be identified as the
author of this work has been asserted by him in accordance
with the Copyright, Designs and Patents Act, 1988

First published in the United Kingdom in 1983 by Orbis Publishing Ltd
Reprinted 1983, 1984, 1985; reprinted by Queen Anne Press 1986, 1988
Second edition published in the United Kingdom in 1989 by Queen Anne Press
Third edition published in the United Kingdom in 1993 by Stanley Paul Limited
Random House, 20 Vauxhall Bridge Road, London SW1V 2SA

Random House Australia (Pty) Limited
20 Alfred Street, Milsons Point, Sydney,
New South Wales 2061, Australia

Random House New Zealand Limited
18 Poland Road, Glenfield,
Auckland 10, New Zealand

Random House South Africa (Pty) Limited
PO Box 337, Bergvlei, South Africa

Random House UK Limited Reg. No. 954009

A CIP catalogue record for this book
is available from the British Library

ISBN 0 09 178188 4

Printed and bound in Great Britain by
Cox & Wyman Ltd, Reading, Berkshire

CONTENTS

PREFACE TO THE SECOND EDITION

It is now some eight years since, in reply to your writer, publishing houses by the dozen expressed the view, 'American Football has little chance of catching on and we regret that ...' Thankfully, Orbis Publishing and, subsequently, Macdonald Queen Anne Press took a different view, and the result was the best-selling book of its kind in Europe.

Since the first publication of *Guide* in 1983, the principles of the game have remained unchanged, and it is true that there have been no major innovations of the kind which had significant implications for the use of the forward pass in the late 1970s. However, it is one feature of American Football that it is in constant evolution as the rules makers track the ever-shifting point of equilibrium between offense and defense. There have, then, been several modifications and reinterpretations of existing law. Equally, on the field, coaches have found new ways of attempting to fool the opposition. Passing offenses have become more complex, as have the defensive systems designed to stop the pass. Again, the complexities of the so-called One-Back offense have added bewildering variety to the rushing game.

Restating the original philosophy of *Guide*, which was an attempt to assist beginners in their enjoyment of the game, there are sections of text which are essentially unchanged, simply because many of the explanations and diagrams are as valid now as they were then. For the emerging host of British experts, it is hoped that there will be some value in an update which is meant to be an accurate, yet uncomplicated treatment.

K.T. 1989

INTRODUCTION

American Football is not unlike the codes of rugby football in that the ball is the same shape (prolate spheroid), the goal posts are similar and serve an identical purpose, and players attempt to make forward progress by running with the ball in hand. Furthermore, the principal method of halting the ball-carrier is by tackling. However, in American Football, once the ball-carrier is tackled to the ground, or clearly held, the ball is ruled dead and play comes to a complete halt. It restarts with a set piece, a face-to-face confrontation known formally as a 'scrimmage' but idiomatically as a 'down'. The team in possession is allowed four of these downs. By using one, two, three or all four downs, 10 or more yards must be gained. If this yardage requirement is satisfied, possession is retained and a new set of four downs is earned. By repeatedly gaining the necessary 10 yards within the sequence of the four downs, possession is maintained and the attacking team (known as the 'offense') moves systematically down the field with the eventual object of scoring. If the offense fails to make the necessary 10 yards during a particular four-down series, possession is transferred to the opposition (formerly the 'defense'), which then becomes the attacking team (offense) and embarks on its return drive. This, then, is the basis of the ebb and flow of American Football.

The game takes place on a pitch measuring 360 feet long and 160 feet wide (Fig 1). The choice of width was neither arbitrary nor ordained, but simply was the maximum available to Walter Camp

Fig 1:
The Gridiron.

13

when he set out to formalize the game in the 1880s. It is essential and convenient that the pitch be marked out at intervals of 5 yards and, to a lesser extent, 1 yard. The pitch therefore has the appearance of a 'gridiron', which has become a popular name for it.

The prime objective is to score a 'touchdown', worth 6 points, following which there is a kick at goal worth 1 point, called 'extra point attempt'. There is also the possibility of scoring with a 'field goal kick' (3 points), which can be attempted at all times during the game on any set-piece down, and from any yardage position. The obvious comparison is with a penalty kick at goal in rugby, yet since an infringement by the opposition is *not* a prerequisite, more sensibly it might be compared with a drop-kick at goal, which in rugby too forms part of normal play.

Points can also be scored by forcing the offensive team to concede a 'safety' score (worth 2 points). This is described in Chapter I.

There are several major distinctions between American Football and rugby, the first of which is associated with passing the ball. From every set-piece down, *one* forward pass is allowed (obviously by the offense) and it is worth noting that this pass must be delivered from the attacking team's side of the scrimmage line. In other words, a player in possession cannot hare off downfield and then throw a forward pass.

The second departure from rugby is that deliberate obstruction, known as 'blocking', is quite legal. In doing this, a player is seeking to prevent the opposition from tackling the player of his own team who is carrying the ball. Again, the methods of blocking are strictly regulated and are to be distinguished from 'tackling', which may be considered as using one's arms to encircle and hold an opponent. Significantly, a tackle, as in rugby, can be performed *only* on the player carrying the ball.

Free and unlimited substitution is allowed at all times of the game, between downs, to enable a player to perform his specialist role. In a 47-man squad there can be identified two groups of players, the defensive unit and the offensive unit, and in modern Football it is virtually unknown for a man to play both on offense and defense. One of the first things a new spectator notices, therefore, is the

Helmet

Mouthguard

Facemask

Shoulder pads

Foam collar

Arm pads

Elbow pads

Rib pads

Forearm pads

Hip pads

Jockstrap

Lineman's gloves

Thigh pads

Knee pads

Shin pads

Ankle tape

Fig 2: *Protective equipment.*

constant comings and goings of players, particularly when, following a loss of possession, the offensive unit of a team is replaced by the defensive unit.

Another striking difference from rugby is the use of protective clothing. The players may look rather bizarre as they lumber onto the field, armour glistening in the sun. Yet even with this protection, which can weigh up to 25 lbs, injuries which result in permanent disability still occur. The black-and-white photographs of the good old days, when men were men, reveal players sporting only a dog-eared leather scrum cap for protection. Sadly, in those days fatalities were not uncommon. Football was then, and remains today, a violent game.

It is not to be expected that a single reading of this book will make a newcomer to American Football an instant expert. The intricacies of no worthwhile game could be mastered so easily. But if the reader, after watching a game, returns to the book to identify some of the plays he has seen, then by the end of the season he should be as well informed as most of the long-term fans.

CHAPTER I

SCORING POINTS

THE TOUCHDOWN DRIVE

By successfully gaining 10 or more yards within each four-down series, the team on offense systematically moves the ball downfield until a touchdown is scored. A typical touchdown drive is illustrated by the following sequence of plays, beginning with the team in possession on its own 45-yard line, i.e. 55 yards away from the opposition goal line. Fig 3 shows this sequence diagrammatically.

1st down and 10 yards to go (described in commentaries as 1st and 10):
Play gains 4 yards and so the next down becomes 2nd down and 6 yards to go on the 49-yard line.

2nd down and 6 yards to go (2nd and 6):
Play gains 3 yards and so the next down becomes 3rd down and 3 yards to go on the opponents' 48-yard line.

3rd down and 3 yards to go (3rd and 3):
Play gains 7 yards and so the next down becomes 1st down and 10 yards to go because, by gaining 10 or more yards in three downs, another series of four downs had been earned.

1st and 10 on the 41-yard line:
Play gains 6 yards and so the next down becomes 2nd and 4 from the 35-yard line.

Fig 3: *The touchdown drive.*

2nd and 4 on the 35-yard line:
Play gains 12 yards (more than the 4 yards necessary, hence earning another series of four downs).

1st and 10 on the 23-yard line:
Play gains 14 yards (more than enough for another series of four downs) and the ball is now on the 9-yard line. From this field position, the terminology for the next down changes to become 1st down and Goal to go (1st and Goal) because there remain fewer than 10 yards to go for a touchdown score.

1st and Goal from the 9-yard line:
Play gains 4 yards and so the next down becomes 2nd and Goal from the 5-yard line.

2nd and Goal from the 5-yard line:
Play goes into the end zone for a touchdown.

Note that in the diagram (Fig 3), each play (down) begins with the ball on or within the 'hashmarks'. If a particular play terminates outside the hashmarks, the ball is moved laterally to the closest hashmark for the next down (indicated by a dotted line). If a play terminates at a point within the hashmarks, the next down begins with the ball 'spotted' at that point.

LOSS OF YARDAGE

As will become apparent later, the play from any particular down can result in a loss of yardage. This loss is simply added to the yardage which was required from that particular down to give the yardage needed for another series of four downs. For example:

1st and 10 from the opposition 40-yard line:
Play *loses* 6 yards and so the next down becomes 2nd down and 16 yards to go, from the opposition 46-yard line.

2nd and 16 from the opposition 46-yard line:
Play *loses* 1 yard making the next down 3rd down and 17 from the 47-yard line.

SCORING A TOUCHDOWN

The formal requirements for the award of a touchdown, worth 6 points, are best exemplified by description of the two most common methods, namely 'rushing' and 'passing', by which the score is achieved.

Rushing Touchdown

The ball, which must be under the full control of the ball-carrier (the rusher) needs simply to break the vertical plane which extends directly upwards from the goal line. *The goal line is part of the end zone.* Unlike the requirement for a try in rugby, it is not necessary to

Fig 4: *The imaginary plane representing the front of the end zone.*

place the ball onto the playing surface. To this extent, the term 'touchdown' is misleading.

Passing Touchdown

An offensive player already in the end zone needs to catch and demonstrate his full control of the ball, which usually will have been thrown to him by the quarterback. If, as often happens, he has had to jump to catch the ball, he must land to touch the playing surface, with both feet within the end zone. It must be noted that *the sidelines and the end (back) line are out of bounds* and, therefore, his feet must not touch these lines in his initial contact with the playing surface. There is, however, a supplementary rule which gives an advantage to the pass receiver who catches the ball (not necessarily in the end zone) in the process of being tackled. If, in the opinion of the referee, he would have landed in bounds but was driven out of bounds by the force of the tackle before his feet could touch the ground, the pass reception (touchdown if in the end zone) is allowed.

Obviously a player can score a touchdown by catching the ball within the field of play and running into the end zone, as described for a rushing touchdown.

EXTRA POINT ATTEMPT

Immediately following a touchdown, the offense kicks at goal from directly in front of the posts, the line of scrimmage being the 2-yard line. The kick, if successful, is worth 1 point and 'converts' the touchdown score of 6 to 7 points. A description of the extra point attempt is given in Chapter VII.

FIELD GOAL

On any one of the four downs, at any time, the offense can attempt a kick at goal, from a formal set-piece down. This, worth 3 points, is roughly equivalent to a penalty goal or drop goal in rugby, and will normally be attempted on 4th down, when within sensible range (up to about 35 yards) of the opposition goal line and in circumstances under which the gain of another series of four downs is unlikely (discussed later under PUNTING v FIELD GOAL ATTEMPT). If the kick, say from a down on the opposition 30-yard line, is unsuccessful, possession is transferred and the opposition initiates its counter-attack from that very same 30-yard line which was the original line of scrimmage. For an unsuccessful kick which was from within the opposition 20-yard line, play restarts on the 20-yard line. A description of the field goal attempt is given in Chapter VII.

CONCEDING A SAFETY SCORE

Occasionally, an offensive player will find himself in possession of the ball inside his own end zone. This can occur when the team on offense is deep within its own half. The unfortunate ball-carrier will have been obliged to retreat into the end zone in an attempt to evade the pursuit of defenders. If the defense can trap him inside the end zone, by establishing a firm hold or by tackling him to the ground, a safety score, worth 2 points, is conceded by the offense. Equally, if the ball-carrier can be forced to run over his own end line or sidelines (all of which delineate the end zone), a 2-point safety is conceded. Once the ball-carrier is in the end zone, there is only one legitimate way out and that is in the forward (attacking) direction. To make matters worse, the team conceding the safety must restart play by placekicking or punting from its own 20-yard line, which will always place the opposition in an excellent field position.

PUNTING

Punting is not a method of scoring but is most conveniently discussed in this section. On any one of the four downs, the attacking team can simply punt the ball as far as possible downfield. In doing this, possession is relinquished to the opposition who, on receiving the punted ball, will immediately attempt a return run which experience shows will be restricted on average to 8.5 yards. The objective of the punt is to place the opposition deep in its own half from which position it will begin its formal return drive by the sequence of downs.

However, it is a truism that in Football, as for every other game with the notable exception of grenade catching, possession is of vital importance. It is necessary to add, therefore, that to punt the precious possession away, which might appear an act of gross profligacy is, on the contrary, a safety first and conservative strategy, as will be shown in the following section.

PUNTING v FIELD GOAL ATTEMPT

Let us imagine that the offense has used three downs in gaining 7 yards and yet is still on its own 30-yard line. From the 4th down play, 3 vital yards are necessary to earn another series of four downs and maintain the drive. Failure to gain these 3 yards on 4th down is disastrous, for handing over possession in the region of the 30-yard line is to place the opposition in a very dangerous field position from which to launch the counter-attack. Indeed, to risk transferring possession at any point within one's own half is considered nothing short of lunacy. Additionally, to attempt a field goal kick at goal posts which are barely visible in the unattainable distance, would be an act of equal madness. The conservative team, not willing to risk failure to gain the 3 yards will, on 4th down, punt the ball away. The average net distance gained from a punt, after taking into account an average return run, is approximately 32 yards. In the case of a down on the 30-yard line, it follows that the opposition must start its counter-attack from, say, its own 38-yard line.

The situation is very different for the offense whose drive has come to a halt with just a 4th down left, but this time on the opposition 25-yard line. Again, to punt the ball away is an option but now there exists the possibility of a successful field goal attempt, failure at which would result in no significant positional disadvantage. Under normal circumstances, the offense would attempt the field goal for its reward of 3 points.

It should be mentioned that, for a team on offense yet losing by more than 3 points and with time running out, the kicking options are ignored. All four downs are used in the quest for that elusive touchdown. This results in exciting play, and the fans love it.

CHAPTER II

PLAYER POSITIONS

In the preceding chapter, methods by which the ball can be moved were given little consideration, so as not to obscure the overall view of the workings of the game. To anyone who has seen anything of Football it is trivial to say that these methods involve running with the ball, passing the ball or some combination of the two. A more detailed description of these can be absorbed only by first knowing player positions. The roles of each player in running and passing can then evolve.

THE SQUAD

The choreography of Football seems to require a cast of thousands. However, the reality is that a squad consists of 47 players, 45 of which can be active for a game. Of these, some three or so will take to the field only if both the specialist player and his replacement in a particular position are damaged beyond repair. Otherwise, this fortunate three can view the action from the comfort of the squad bench, hence their 'title' of 'bench warmers'. Unlimited substitution is allowed at all times between plays, but at any one time a team will have only eleven players on the field. This will be the 'offensive unit', the 'defensive unit' or the 'special team'. Of these three, it is the special team whose role is least obvious. At this stage, it is necessary to say only that they will play in situations involving kicking, i.e. at the beginning of each half, for a field goal attempt, when punting or to restart after a score.

THE OFFENSIVE UNIT

The offensive unit in one of several standard formations is shown in Fig 5.

It is a legal requirement that there be *at least* seven players to form the 'offensive line', the limits of which are defined by the players at the extreme ends. In the example shown, these players are the 'wide receiver' and the 'tight end'. Excluding these, the five grouped together, namely the 'tackles', 'guards' and 'center', constitute the 'interior line'. Interior linemen are primarily guardians. They are the 'heavies' who protect the 'quarterback' or pave the way for the ball-carrier, who will almost always be a 'running back' or occasionally, the quarterback. The wide receiver and 'flanker' are primarily pass receivers. The quarterback directs the show by 'handing off' the ball to a running back or throwing a pass to a receiver. Of all eleven players, the tight end has to be perhaps the most versatile, playing on the one hand the role of interior lineman and on the other that of pass receiver.

So much then for the positions of the offensive unit and briefly considered responsibilities of the players who occupy them.

Fig 5: *Offensive unit: pro set formation*.

WR = Wide receiver	TE	= Tight end
T = Tackle	Fl	= Flanker
G = Guard	QB	= Quarterback
C = Center	RB	= Running back

THE DEFENSIVE UNIT

The defensive unit confronts the offensive unit and can also adopt many standard formations, one of which is shown in Fig 6.

The three defensive players, 'ends' and 'nose tackle', who line up face to face with the offensive line, constitute the 'defensive line' and will primarily attempt to ward off the aggressive intentions of the offensive line before tackling the ball-carrier. The four 'defensive backs' who are the 'cornerbacks' and 'safeties', have a responsibility to defend against the pass. The 'linebackers', two outside and two inside, are required to identify the offensive play as either rushing or passing, before reacting to tackle the ball-carrier or assist the defensive backs in defending against the pass.

It is important to note that whereas movement of offensive players, immediately prior to the start of each play, is restricted (this is discussed later), players on defense are free to move around at will. Indeed, this they will do, particularly linebackers and safeties, in the attempt to create confusion for the offense. Typically, a safety and

Fig 6: *The defensive unit: 3–4–4 formation.*

E = Defensive end   S = Safety
T = Nose tackle   CB = Cornerback
LB = Linebacker

Fig 7: *Defensive unit immediately prior to the start of a down.*

two cornerbacks might line up close to the line of scrimmage to await the start of play, before adjusting to defensive positions. Thus, the defensive unit may resemble the arrangement shown in Fig 7.

THE COMPOSITION OF A SQUAD

Almost without exception, every player in Professional Football will have spent four years in College Football. Far from being a market-place free-for-all, entry into the professional ranks is rigidly controlled. All graduating college seniors are placed in a pool from which the professional clubs make selections in the order determined by their previous season's playing record. This is called the 'collegiate draft' and takes place in late April. The club with the worst record is given the first selection and the Super Bowl winner the last. Thus, in round one, 28 players are chosen. There are 12 rounds in all, selection in each one following the same order.

It may seem unfair on the best college player to be drafted by the worst club and it usually takes around a million dollars to ease the hurt. The arguments in favour of this system rest on the belief that, over a period of time, the playing strengths of each club will approach parity. Equally, the weakest club is virtually guaranteed a superstar from the draft, while no club with bottomless coffers can corner the market.

Not all college players will be selected. The unlucky ones who still wish to play professionally must travel from club to club, trying to impress coaches on the practice field. Some of those formally drafted will be released to join these so-called 'free agents' doing the rounds. There is severe competition for a place in the allowed number of 47 players per club.

Established players can of course be transferred, yet even here it is rare for cash to change hands. Rather, the arrangement involves the exchange of players, sometimes together with draft options. Thus a club entitled to a prime draft selection can transfer this option to another club, in exchange for an established player of high standing.

A 47-man squad will consist typically of the following:

Quarterbacks	2-3	Defensive linemen	6-7
Running backs	5-6	Linebackers	6-7
Wide receivers	4-5	Defensive backs	8-9
Tight ends	3	Kicker	1
Offensive linemen	8-9	Punter	1

NUMBERING OF PLAYERS

All players wear a shirt, numbered on the front, back and upper arm. This is not so much for the obvious reason – that of player identification – but more to indicate the *position* he will occupy and the role he will play. This is important in enforcement of the rules as each player, with some exceptions, is allowed to perform only certain acts. For example, interior offensive linemen are not allowed to receive a forward pass. The officials can easily spot a culprit by the number on his shirt. He may change his assignment to that of pass receiver, but only by informing the referee prior to the start of a particular play. The player positions, together with the range of numbers allowed, are as follows:

Quarterbacks, kickers and punters (all offense)	1-19
Running backs (offense), cornerbacks and safeties (defense)	20-49
Centers (offense) and linebackers (defense)	50-59
Centers, interior linemen (offense) and defensive linemen	60-79
Tight ends, wide receivers and flankers (offense)	80-89
Further defensive linemen and linebackers	90-99

CHAPTER III

OFFENSIVE PLAY

For anyone who has seen Football on television, however casually, some concept of an offensive play will have been gained. It will probably run as follows: 'One of the front linemen gives the ball to the quarterback who then retreats, before handing the ball to a runner, or throwing a pass.' This chapter will consider these basic processes and their subsequent developments.

The obvious place to start is with the quarterback, for he is the glittering star whose exploits, both on and off the field, are most often discussed. Or should it be with the running back, who is probably the most highly paid and around whom, traditionally, a Football team is built? One could establish a case for the wide receiver, whose blazing speed and magnificent hands will almost certainly have been featured in the pre-telecast promotion. Yet the reputations of these players can be built only on the foundation of a rock-like interior line, in the absence of which the offensive unit will be routed, so let us start with this.

THE INTERIOR LINE

The story, indeed the playing action, begins with the quarterback virtually straddling the center and barking out signals (these are understood only by members of his own team and are best considered as a countdown to the moment when the quarterback intends to begin the play). At a particular moment, pre-arranged in

Fig 8: *Center 'snapping' ball to quarterback.*

the 'huddle', the center 'snaps' the ball to the quarterback (see Fig 8) who, now at the controls, continues the play.

It is the choice of this play, either to run or to pass, which determines the responsibilities of the center in concert with his interior linemen. What is for certain is that, at all times, their job is to protect the ball-carrier whoever he may be. This they will do using

Fig 9: *Illegal block from behind and below the waist, known as 'clipping'.*

nothing less than deliberate obstruction. Technically known as 'blocking', this is quite legal and can be performed to varying degrees by every player on the field. There are two legal variations of blocking, depending upon whether the play is a rush or a pass. On a rushing play, the offensive lineman is somewhat restricted in the use of his hands and arms. He can extend his arms but, essentially, he uses his body momentum. On passing plays, he enjoys greater freedom in that he can extend his arms, with hands open, to keep his opponent at bay. However, he is not allowed to use his hands in an attempt to grab and hold. Additionally, for reasons of safety, any part of an opponent from the neck upwards, including his helmet and facemask, is forbidden territory. More heinous even than this is the illegal block from behind and below the waist, known as 'clipping', and shown in Fig 9. This act of treachery invokes the maximum response, short of sending-off, by way of penalty.

Interior Linemen on Passing Plays

Immediately the ball is snapped, the interior line must make an initial and ferocious hit on the defensive line, which it is likely to outnumber. This is rapidly followed by a collective and gradual retreat to form a protective 'pocket', from which temporary sanctuary the quarterback can await developments before delivering his pass. The protection pocket is shown in Fig 10.

Once in position, the interior lineman must hold his ground in the face of the onslaught from defensive linemen, linebackers and perhaps a safety. For a passing play of any magnitude, the quarterback needs a minimum of three seconds to allow for his pass receivers to run downfield, and clearly this 'pocket time' may be taken as a measure of the effectiveness of the interior line. A pocket

Fig 10: *Quarterback in pass protection pocket. The wide receiver, running back and flanker have moved out to be in position to catch a pass.*

time greater than three seconds shifts the advantage heavily in favour of the quarterback, while anything less than two seconds adds up to disaster. In 12 of the first 23 Super Bowls, quarterbacks were voted Most Valuable Player. But this may be as much a vote for the time they were given by their offensive linemen as it was for their abilities in passing a football.

An alternative strategy on passing plays might conceivably be for the interior line, with its numerical superiority, to obliterate the defensive line at the line of scrimmage. For two reasons, one legal and the other tactical, this does not happen. First, on a play resulting in a forward pass, the interior linemen are not allowed to travel more than one yard beyond the line of scrimmage until *after* the ball leaves the passer's hand. It follows that the forward momentum gathered by the interior lineman, and delivered in the initial collision, must be controlled so as not to infringe this law. Secondly, a defense alerted to expect a pass play will reinforce its defensive line with linebackers, and perhaps a safety, taking closer order. Defensive players, then in superior numbers, would almost certainly find their way around the ends of the offensive protective line. The formation of a pocket is the natural adjustment to counteract this.

Interior Linemen on Rushing Plays

On receiving the snapped ball, the quarterback takes two or three steps away from the line and 'hands off' the ball to a runner. Back at the line of scrimmage, the clatter of helmets to a background strain of grunts signals that the battle to create a gap is under way. It is towards this turbulence and mayhem that the ball-carrier rushes.

In one sense, on passing plays the role of an offensive lineman is the passive one of wait-and-see before reacting. On the other hand, his part in rushing plays is an altogether different business – he can now go to war. He must dominate his opponent. This he will do by hitting the man in an upward direction and raising him to the point beyond which he is betrayed by his own centre of gravity, as shown in Fig 11.

This achieved, the forward drive, generated by enormous leg power, must be maintained and the opponent shoved to this side or

Fig 11: *Offensive lineman (No 54) blocks defensive player (No 60).*

that, to create the gap through which the ball-carrier will rush, as illustrated in Fig 12.

Success depends not merely on strength, for this will be matched, but rather on its application with perfect timing and at the correct angle of rise. The offensive lineman has the advantage in timing since he knows the precise moment at which the ball will be snapped. However, if his upward angle of thrust is not correct his momentum will be misdirected (too high or too low) and the contest, being inconclusive at best, will represent a loss to the offense. For out of stalemate at the line of scrimmage, the defense emerges the winner since the offense has been restricted to little or no gain in yardage.

As an alternative to the frontal assault, the play may be designed to run around the end of the offensive line. In this case, an interior lineman assumes the role of travelling guardian. Closely following the snap and rather than confronting his opposite number, the guard will pull away from the line to sweep around the end, leading the

Fig 12: *Creation of a gap in defensive line: blocking by right guard and right tackle. The running back aims for the gap between right guard and right tackle.*

ball-carrier into open field. Now on the rampage and towing his running back, he needs to execute a clean block on the approaching defender, usually a linebacker or safety, thus releasing the ball-carrier for further gain. For a play directed to the right side, either the right or left guard might pull away from the line to lead the rush, as shown in Figs 13 and 14.

There is little doubt that much of the success achieved by the great running back is attributable to the blocking protection of his offensive guard. Running behind Reggie McKenzie, O.J. Simpson of Buffalo became a legend in the early 1970s. For the remainder of the decade, the story was that of Pittsburgh's Franco Harris breaking all Super Bowl records behind the blocking of, first, Jim Clack, and then Sam Davis. In the 1980s, the Cowboys' Tony Dorsett was catapulted into open field by the blocking of Herb Scott while the Rams' Eric Dickerson was helped greatly in the early days of his career by Kent Hill.

It is a natural sequence, then, that following the consideration of the role of the offensive lineman should be that of the running back.

Fig 13: *Right guard leads rush down right side*.

Fig 14: *Left guard leads rush down right side*.

THE RUNNING BACK

From its beginning, Football was traditionally a running (rushing) game. However, the successive rule changes of the 1970s have shifted the balance in favour of the passing offense. The running back still plays an important part for he too is a legal pass receiver. This aspect of his game is discussed more appropriately under the heading of PASS RECEIVERS; here we deal with his role as ball-carrier.

In simple terms, the quarterback 'hands off' to a running back who will try to gain yardage either through or around the offensive line. A normal offensive unit will field two running backs who will take up positions some four yards behind the offensive line, as in Fig 15.

Fig 15: *Running backs identified by* ⊗.

The Frontal Assault

In theory, on receipt of the ball, the runner will rush towards that part of the line at which a gap will have been created by his linemen. The playing reality might be, however, an altogether different business. Far less than a definite gap, it is more likely to be a barely discernible chink of daylight, a seam. It is through this that the runner must penetrate. Furthermore this seam might well materialize in an unexpected part of the line. In his 4-yard build-up the runner must therefore be reading the effectiveness of his interior linemen before exploiting the opportunities gained by their efforts. With maximum force, head down and shoulder pointing, he hits the seam and takes whatever yardage he can, together with the inevitable beating. From the resulting pile-up the officials will decide, one way or another, that he has gained 1, perhaps 2 yards. So it's 2nd and 8 yards to go with less than 45 seconds on the clock (see Chapter IX) before the next play must begin. He stoops in the collective huddle, head still ringing, to hear the quarterback call the next play: 'Okay guys, same again'.

Of course it isn't always like this for he can reasonably expect that, say, once in four times, a reasonable gap will be there, but even so there will still be opposition. Having cleared the line of scrimmage, he will be confronted by a linebacker. However, there is now some help available; the other running back has not been standing idly by. When the gap opens his responsibility is to lead the ball-carrier much as would an offensive guard. A clean block on the linebacker by this lead blocker will spring the ball-carrier into open field where he can now wreak havoc. A 15-yard gain is possible and, against a defense which has erred in placing its safety wide and at the line of scrimmage, a 50-yard touchdown run is not uncommon. This block by the second running back is shown in Fig 16.

Fig 16: *Running back blocks for ball-carrier.*

Such then are the fluctuating tasks and fortunes of a running back in making a frontal assault. Should he choose the attack around the end of the line, a similar situation exists.

Around the End (The Sweep Play)

After an initial 1-yard move in a forward direction, the ball-carrier in an around-the-end play will veer off to one side, hoping to exploit an open field weakness. The initial forward move is made in an effort to influence linebackers to hold position behind their offensive line, which would be normal in defense against a frontal attack. If the linebackers are fooled, the chances of success are increased dramatically. Again, a great deal depends on the outside blocking protection the ball-carrier will receive, now from perhaps both a guard and tackle together with the other running back, shown in Fig 17.

Fig 17: *A run around the end with blocking by tackle, running back and pulling guard.*

If the defense is not fooled the play will make little gain. The lead blocking trio will be swamped by linebackers crossing to cover and the two safeties advancing to assist. In all likelihood, the ball-carrier will be forced over the sideline for little or no gain. The successful cover is shown in Fig 18.

It may be self-evident that the alternative tactics of a frontal assault and an end run require of the running back different physical qualities. Indeed, the most effective pairs are those in which one has power and durability and the other brilliant speed and agility. Such a combination was that of Larry Csonka and Eugene 'Mercury' Morris, in the early 1970s. With Csonka going up the middle and Morris around the end, Miami dominated the NFL for two seasons and well into a third. Such combinations are, however, rare, and a team will

Fig 18: *Linebackers, safety and cornerback cover an end run.*

normally possess just one outstanding running back. Following Csonka and Morris, only twice have two players from one team rushed for 1,000-or-more yards in the same season. They are Pittsburgh's Franco Harris and Rocky Bleier (1976), and the Cleveland pairing of Kevin Mack and Earnest Byner (1985). In a 16-game regular season, perhaps a dozen rushers will break the 1,000-yard barrier, averaging around 4.5 yards per attempt. The real workhorses, such as Eric Dickerson (Colts), Joe Morris (Giants), Herschel Walker (Cowboys) and Roger Craig (49ers), will carry the ball more than 20 times each game. And it is hardly surprising that many running backs undergo major knee surgery. In support of the star, there will be two or three lesser lights, some still cutting their teeth and others past their best, who will grind out a modest 300-or-so yards at an average of not much better than three yards per attempt when not on blocking duty. At this end of the spectrum, Football is less than glamorous. Still, the breakaway run for a touchdown is a spectacular sight and happens with such explosive pace that one is advised not to blink. Several NFL running backs, the most prominent of recent years being Herschel Walker, have competed with distinction in international sprints. It may be that the Raiders' Bo Jackson is even faster than Walker.

PASS RECEIVERS

One major departure from rugby in the rules of American Football, namely the legality of deliberate obstruction, has previously been discussed. Another is that the ball may be passed in any direction, including forwards. Unlike lateral passes and those in a backward direction, which can be made at any part of the field, the forward pass can be made only from behind the line of scrimmage. Furthermore, only one forward pass is allowed. It can be thrown by any player from behind the line but in practice is usually thrown by the quarterback. The forward pass may be caught by those two players who line up at the extreme ends of the offensive line, and additionally by all those who, at the snap of the ball, are standing more than one yard back from the line of scrimmage. These so-called 'eligible receivers' are shown in Fig 19.

Fig 19: *Eligible receivers marked by* ⊗.

If the ball is not caught, the play is ruled as an 'incomplete pass'. The game clock is stopped and play resumes at the original line of scrimmage but with the loss of that particular down. For example, say on 2nd down and 10 from the 45-yard line, a forward pass is not caught (incomplete). The next play becomes 3rd down and 10 from that very same 45-yard line.

Passing plays are conveniently described under three headings: short, medium and long.

The Short Pass

The short pass is used in circumstances when only 2 or 3 yards are required to gain another 1st down. It is usually directed towards the sideline and only rarely over the middle. As a valuable alternative to the running play, especially with defensive players massed in the middle area, it gives width to an offense and allows the receiver to read the distribution of the defense before threading his way downfield. For the short pass, a running back is usually the intended receiver. Fig 20 shows the positional play.

Fig 20: *Running back takes up position for short pass. The tackles, guards and center form a temporary pocket, together with one running back. Wide receiver, tight end and flanker make decoy runs, with defensive backs and linebackers almost certainly dropping back to cover.*

To use a running back in this way has been a significant and noticeable tactical development of modern football and it is not uncommon for him to make four receptions in a game, gaining, on average, 8 yards per catch. As always for a sizeable gain, lead blockers are indispensable. These will be the other running back, the tight end and the guard pulling away from the line of scrimmage, shown in Fig 21.

The Medium Pass
With the medium pass, we come to the specialist pass receivers who take up wide positions on or behind the line of scrimmage. Classically,

Fig 21: *Blocking for running back receiving short pass. The guard, tackles and center form a temporary pocket. Wide receiver and flanker make decoy runs with some defensive players dropping back to cover. Running back adopts a lateral position to make the reception, allowing blockers to take up stations.*

there are two types of pass, one down the sideline, the other over the middle. The medium pass down the sideline is simplicity itself. In execution, the intended receiver runs down the sideline, stops, turns his back to the defending cornerback and makes the reception. By turning, he effectively shields the ball, thus guarding against an interception by the defender. This manoeuvre is shown in Fig 22.

For the play to succeed, the stop and turn must be in rapid sequence and after instant and yet heavily disguised deceleration by the runner, previously travelling at maximum speed. A gentle slowing down would reveal the play to the marking cornerback who will not need a second hint. Having made the reception, the receiver will attempt to make forward progress, almost certainly by cutting infield and, alas for him, into the welcoming arms of the safety. It is perhaps the weakness of the sideline pass that the receiver is hemmed in by this very sideline. On the other hand the sideline can represent salvation for both him and his team. First, by stepping out of bounds he will avoid the savage tackle from the cornerback whose area has been violated. Additionally, for a team losing and with time running out, by

Fig 22: *Medium pass down the sideline: the hook pattern. The quarterback drops back in the pass pocket. Wide receiver and tight end run decoy patterns.*

stepping over the sideline he can stop the game clock.

For a defensive alignment which has its linebackers tightly in support of the defensive line and its safeties lying back to defend against the long pass, there is a no-man's-land. It is this that the medium range pass over the middle is designed to exploit, as shown in Fig 23.

The pass trajectory will need to be such as to clear the line of scrimmage and inevitably the ball will be caught by the receiver leaping high into the air, as Fig 24 shows. Having been watching the

Fig 23: *Medium pass over the middle. The quarterback is in the pass pocket. Tight end and flanker run decoy patterns. Two linebackers and the defensive backs, recognizing a pass play, have dropped back to cover.*

evolving pass play and by now recovering to defend, the safety will deliver a crushing tackle on the receiver who, with both feet off the ground, exposes himself to the risk of severe injury, particularly to his back. It is a feat of great skill in catching and an act of extreme courage for the receiver who, by retaining control of the ball until grounded, completes the reception. This thorax of a defense is no place for the faint-hearted.

Fig 24: *Wide receiver catches pass in heavy traffic.*

The Long Pass

This most difficult pass to execute, the long pass is spectacular and dramatic, and is the killer strike. On completion, a pass receiver with even the least sense of occasion will stride majestically into the end zone, ball triumphantly held aloft in acknowledgement of the pandemonium from the stands. The so-called 'bomb' pass will be delivered to coincide with the arrival of the receiver who will have run

Fig 25: *Long pass to deep middle or corner. The quarterback is in the pass pocket. Wide receiver runs the flag pattern (i.e. towards the corner). Flanker runs the post pattern (i.e. towards the posts).*

either close to the corner or over the middle and deep, as shown in Fig 25.

The route taken by the pass receiver, not always direct, is known as his pass pattern. This he will run for the greater part, not looking for the ball until the last few feet of its flight. To turn his head prematurely would alert the defender who could well be in close contact and keeping pace.

In a section devoted to offensive play such as this, the opportunities open to a defense have been omitted for clarity and reserved for later. But with both wide receiver and cornerback homing in on the ball, it would be quite wrong to defer discussion of the defensive option. Simply, once the ball is in the air it belongs to whomsoever can catch it. It is a major achievement if the defense can intercept the pass, for not only will a touchdown have been prevented but they can immediately counter-attack. However, in attempting to catch the ball, any illegal contact which would take the form of bumping and holding, by either player, is severely penalized. Pass interference by the offense nullifies any gain which may otherwise have been made (discussed in the Rules section). For a guilty defense, the penalty is the award of an automatic 1st down to the offense, with play restarting at the point of infringement.

The wide receiver and flanker will almost certainly possess searing pace; indeed a track time greater than 10.5 seconds for 100 metres is considered slow. The retired Bob Hayes of the Dallas Cowboys was an Olympic sprint champion while both Johnny 'Lam' Jones (Jets) and Ron Brown (Rams) won gold medals in 4×100 metres sprint relay teams. Current Raider Willie Gault is a hurdler of world class calibre. The NFL is littered with speedsters who never bothered to compete seriously on the track. Yet speed in itself is not enough, for to it must be added the ability to catch the ball, under both the attention of defenders and the pressures of the occasion. There are, too, a select few players who graced the game and yet were 'slower than the fastest'. Seattle's Steve Largent may well be the slowest of all the current NFL starters, but he is the all-time leader in each of receptions and yardage, and the active leader in touchdowns.

THE TIGHT END

With the possible exception of quarterback, there is no playing position in football which demands more in the way of physical presence and technical skills than the position of tight end. In consecutive plays, he may have to block like an offensive tackle, lead like a guard, take a medium pass in the congested middle area or sprint to the end zone to receive a bomb. The standard dimensions of a tight end are six feet four inches tall and closer to 17 than 16 stones in weight.

As a blocking lineman, his job on running plays is to anchor the offensive line and in particular, for running plays around the end, to 'turn in', thus blocking off an avenue of pursuit, as shown in Fig 26.

Fig 26: *Tight end blocking on running plays around the end.*

As a blocker on passing plays, he is a key element in the evolving pass protection pocket. His assignment will be to control the defensive end, shown in Fig 27.

Fig 27: *Tight end in the pass protection pocket.*

Fig 28: *Tight end runs for pass over the middle. Wide receiver and flanker act as decoys.*

As a pass receiver, he is in no way restricted to a particular pass pattern but his height clearly makes him the most suitable target for the medium pass over the middle and into the teeth of trouble. This is shown in Fig 28, and is not unlike drawing the short straw.

It is a feature of the modern game that this aspect of the tight end's play, pass receiving, assumes even greater importance than ever before. Players such as Mickey Shuler (Jets), Mark Bavaro (Giants), Steve Jordan (Vikings), Keith Jackson (Eagles) and Todd Christensen (Raiders) are maintaining the momentum of an evolving tradition.

THE QUARTERBACK

It may be of some surprise to the reader that in the discussion of offensive plays, only when approaching the final stages does the quarterback appear under the microscope. It would be quite wrong for it to be inferred that he is the least important player. On the contrary, nothing would succeed without his skills. In those things which we have considered, he is at the nerve centre.

The prime requirement of a quarterback is intelligence. Other individual players will have particular assignments and to complete them successfully is to do their jobs. Yet the quarterback must be constantly monitoring the collective result of these separate components before exploiting the opportunities by releasing the ball. He needs the vision of both depth and width in order to take in, simultaneously, these complex interactions. Having done this, he must transfer the ball with a timing in which there is no margin for error.

His active playing duties conveniently resolve into four areas: to hand off to a running back, to pass to a receiver, to run with the ball himself and, in the absence of a sensible alternative, to 'scramble'. Before these, however, he has to go through the starting count drill leading up to the snap of the ball.

The Starting Count Drill

Before each down, the offensive unit goes into a collective huddle to allow the quarterback to explain the next play. The players then take up positions and the quarterback, now straddling the center, begins the formal starting count. A full count would sound something like the following:

'Red 36, Red 36, Set, Hut(1), Hut(2), Hut(3).'

The colour-number code, Red 36, is to confirm to his own players that the prearranged play is still on. Following the 'Set', offensive linemen must remain motionless. To coincide with one of the 'Hut' signals, 1, 2 or 3, the specific 'Hut' being known only by the offensive unit, the center snaps the ball and all hell breaks loose.

Occasionally, once at the line of scrimmage and having read the disposition of defensive players, the quarterback may feel that the chosen play will not succeed. He will alter the play, *at the line of scrimmage*, by changing the colour-number code. The count would then become:

'Red 36, Red 36, Blue 22, Blue 22, Set, Hut(1), Hut(2), Hut(3).'

The whole of the offensive unit will of course be aware that 'Blue 22' signals a late change and, equally, the new play to which 'Blue 22' refers.

Running Plays (Rushing Plays)

The quarterback's part on rushing plays is, perhaps, the most simple of his duties. He needs merely to hand the ball to a running back. Yet even here, his movements leading up to the handoff can be of great assistance to the runner. With the subtlety of his movements as he eases back into position and by pretending to hand the ball to one runner before handing off to another (faking), he can momentarily confuse the linebackers, who can react with full confidence only when the play has been read with certainty. The handoff itself must be with tender loving care since a fumbled ball can be recovered by anyone, including the defense, from the ensuing shambles. With the handoff successfully completed, he will make a discreet withdrawal. He is allowed to block opponents, but, for a player of his strategic importance and relatively flimsy padding, it would be to take a needless risk of injury.

Passing Plays

It is on passing plays that the quarterback earns his bonus, and for these the quality of his throwing arm must be beyond question. He will throw a 20-yard pass with little or no arc in flight, or alternatively hit a target 50 yards away and moving. Again, by his movements as he drops back to pass (play action) he can lure the defensive secondary from its deep cover position, thus giving his wide receivers an edge. On every passing play, there will be both a primary and a secondary receiver, the latter becoming the target only if the former is effectively covered. Should both players be inaccessible, the quarterback will look for another eligible receiver, usually a running back, who will have taken up a position of little strategic importance and yet free from defensive cover. This running back, known as the 'safety-valve', will function simply to allow the quarterback to get rid of the ball, as shown in Fig 29.

Bootlegging

There are occasions when the quarterback will assume the role of ball-carrier in that, rather than handing the ball to a specialist running back, he will hare off into an open space. This is known as

Fig 29: *Running back acts as safety-valve. The quarterback is in the pass pocket but all downfield receivers are marked.*

'bootlegging'. He will attempt to gain rushing yardage but always in anticipation of the impending tackle, before which he will voluntarily go to ground or hop over the sideline. It is valuable as a surprise tactic, and typically a quarterback will average six yards on two or three attempts per game. However, as with blocking, rushing is a bruising business which carries with it the high risk of injury. The thoroughbred quarterback is far too valuable to make a habit of it.

Scrambling
By courtesy of his offensive linemen, the quarterback will operate from a pocket, and with luck, this will remain intact for up to three seconds. However, even the most secure pocket will eventually collapse, and with defenders pouring through gaping holes, this

pocket, designed for his protection, becomes the place of his entrapment. For the quarterback with nowhere to run and all receivers marked, all is not yet lost. Using what might be called a 'professional alternative' (i.e. by bending the rules) he can pass in the direction of a legal receiver and yet deliberately under- or overthrow to enable the ball to bounce harmlessly for an incomplete pass. As described previously, possession is retained and play restarts from the original line of scrimmage on the next down. However, should the referee adjudge that the ball was thrown to ground, with no receivers within 5 yards of the ball, purely to avoid being tackled for a loss of yards ('sacked'), the offense will be penalized by a loss of 10 yards *and* a loss of down. If the quarterback in danger of being sacked disregards this devious ploy, he can run for his life – he can 'scramble'. He does not want to be tackled for a loss of yards; indeed he does not want to be tackled at all. He will therefore scramble around in a most undignified manner, before hopefully escaping to safety over the sideline.

Leadership

It is this aspect of his makeup which is, perhaps, the quarterback's greatest quality. He really must have clear powers of leadership – charisma – for just about every member of the offense, at some time in a game, may have to give his all simply to give Chuck Superstar the chance to go out and claim the glory. The requirements go far beyond simply being a superb athlete – leading by example. In the huddle, when a team is taking a licking and spirits are low, it's his job to convince his teammates that they can overcome the odds. The late Bobby Layne did it as the leader of a hell-raising bunch of carousers. It is an understatement that the late Norm Van Brocklin adopted a more draconian approach. Whatever it takes, the quarterback has to be the unchallenged leader of the pack, for anything less isn't enough.

CHAPTER IV

DEFENSIVE PLAY

Earlier in this book the defensive players were briefly introduced. The diagram (Fig 6) illustrating their playing positions was purposely exaggerated to establish clearly that a defense consists of three elements: linemen, linebackers and defensive backs. Though it is a simplification, this model will be retained for its value in supporting the descriptions of players' responsibilities. It is worth repeating that, immediately prior to the snap, linebackers and safeties may well adopt positions close to the defensive line. Yet it remains true that, regardless of the initial positions they adopt, their defensive responsibilities are essentially unchanged.

DEFENSE AGAINST A RUNNING PLAY

The Frontal Assault

The offensive linemen will be attempting to establish a gap for the running back. As will become apparent from subsequent sections, it is often possible for a defense to anticipate with confidence the type of offensive play it will face. On other occasions, though, it will be a matter of allowing the offense to initiate a play before reacting to defend. This is particularly true for linebackers and defensive backs. The defensive lineman, on the other hand, knows for certain that he will be in collision with offensive linemen on every play, whether it be run or pass. The instant play begins, the defensive lineman will therefore need to absorb this initial contact and very rapidly read the play as run or pass. On a running play, the subject of this section, the offensive lineman is *not* restricted in his downfield movement, and his commitment to a forward and unqualified surge will quickly be detected by the defensive lineman as signalling this running play. His first tasks are not to lose ground, to fight against being shifted to one side or the other, and to prevent the creation of a gap. Should these objectives be achieved and the offensive surge controlled, there is the opportunity for counter-attack by penetrating the offensive line, now in some disarray, to tackle the ball-carrier, not yet at the line of scrimmage, for a loss of yards.

It is a most unlikely event for the defensive linemen alone, outnumbered as they are, to achieve such a success, but of course they are never alone. Immediately the play has been identified as a rush, the linebackers will spring into action, plugging a gap should it appear, or penetrating a weak spot in the offensive line to tackle the ball-carrier. There will even be extra assistance from safeties for they too, having identified the play as a rush, will rapidly advance, as shown in Fig 30.

Fig 30: *Linebackers and safeties defend against the rush*.

57

Fig 31: *Defensive ends charge running backs from around end of line.*

The physical requirements of a defensive lineman are obvious. Dismissing all talk of size and weight, the defensive tackle is best described as an enormous brute. The defensive end is all of this and

Fig 32: *Defensive end tackles quarterback.*

usually equipped with respectable speed, since for him there is always the possibility of charging the running back or quarterback from around the end of the line, as shown in Fig 31, with the desired result shown in Fig 32.

The linebacker is the hunter-killer who, never taking his eyes off the ball-carrier, will attack with reckless abandon. Fig 33 shows a linebacker alert and ready for action.

Fig 33: *The linebacker in 'ready' position.*

Defensive backs are always fast and must be able to execute a clean open-field tackle, since theirs will be the responsibility to bring down not a faltering, barging runner in a melee but rather the man freed from his shackles and approaching maximum speed.

So much, then, for defending against the frontal assault. For a running attack around the end, the attempted penetration will focus some 5 yards or more to one side, along the line of scrimmage. For the defense, the emphasis changes to become one of speed of reaction and pursuit.

The End Run

The defense must react to confront an offense attempting to shift the point of attack away from the congested middle and hoping to profit from surprise. Indeed, with this advantage, the early indications often are that the offense will succeed. Yet to set up a blocking pattern using pulling offensive linemen and perhaps a flanker, and to reach the advantage line (scrimmage line), takes time. In the early stages of the attack, defensive linemen will be left temporarily isolated at the scrimmage, and delayed on the near side by the tight end. Linebackers, however, will detect the play and begin the cross-field move to defend, as shown in Fig 34.

Fig 34: *Linebackers and safety react to an end run. Left guard pulls to right side to lead the runner. Wide receiver runs decoy pattern.*

There are occasions when the alert linebacker, anticipating or sensing the play before its commencement, will direct colleagues to the point of attack. With good reaction timing, a wall of linebackers, reinforced perhaps by two safeties, will force the ball-carrier laterally and ultimately out of bounds, as shown in Fig 35.

If the cross-field cover is established more quickly even than this, the ball-carrier will be forced to seek a route by turning inside and into the clutches of defensive linemen arriving belatedly on the scene. An end run, if successful, is a magnificent expression of collective offensive power, but should it fail, it is a lingering death for the running back.

Fig 35: *Linebackers and safety have anticipated end run.*

DEFENSE AGAINST A PASSING PLAY

For a short pass in the middle area, the responsibility for defending falls to the linebackers, but for all other passes the defensive backs go to work. These are the four players, two safeties and two cornerbacks, who are out-and-out pass defenders and on whom this discussion is primarily centred.

There are two major philosophies of pass defense. The first of these involves the close marking of all pass receivers, 'man for man'; the second is to guard open spaces, the 'zone defense'. The latter is best

Fig 36: *Man-for-man marking. The opposing players are linked by dotted lines.*

seen as evolving from the former and therefore it is appropriate that 'man for man' receives first consideration.

Man for Man

In the normal offensive formation, illustrated in Fig 36, there are five potential pass receivers. Of these, four will be marked by the defensive backs with the fifth and least likely receiver picked up by a linebacker.

The defensive backs will try to establish close contact with their assigned receivers immediately the offensive linemen drop back from the line of scrimmage, signalling a passing play. Safety (1) closely marks the tight end while safety (2) will take up close order with the advancing running back. For the safeties then, it is a question of waiting before acting. On the other hand, the cornerbacks, who are marking wide receivers, have the option to play 'bump and run', described as follows. Within 5 yards of the line of scrimmage, the cornerbacks are allowed to make one blocking contact with the receivers, opposite whom they line up. When play begins and *before the ball is in the air*, the cornerback can block the receiver to the ground, the object being to delay the receiver at the line of scrimmage. This initial block is, however, a risky business for if the cornerback should stumble, the receiver who can avoid the block will escape into open field, unmarked and leaving the cornerback stranded at the line of scrimmage. More often the cornerback, discarding the risk, will seek to establish and maintain body contact, constantly adjusting position, and by this gentler and more subtle art of obstruction, delay the receiver.

There comes a stage, however, when this jostling moves out of the 5-yard area and the quarterback is winding up for the pass. It now becomes a chase. The receiver will hare off on his downfield pass pattern with the cornerback in close contact and running stride for stride. With both players homing in on the ball, decision time for the cornerback is fast approaching.

His prime responsibility is to prevent the pass completion, and this he will do by knocking the ball to the ground (he will bat the ball away). The pass is incomplete, the ball is ruled dead and play will restart with the next down, back at the original line of scrimmage. This is the no-nonsense, safety-first, procedure. Alternatively, at all times the cornerback can attempt to intercept the pass and this he might do by stepping or jumping in front of the receiver, at the last possible moment. Fig 37 shows a defensive back competing for the ball. An interception attempt carries the risk that he may deflect the ball, which can still be caught by the receiver. He may even miss the ball completely and disastrously. Nevertheless, on average, a corner-back will make four interceptions in a season and there is always the possibility of the moment of triumph, the glorious interception return for a touchdown.

There remains a third choice, which is used when the wide receiver has manufactured space for himself and is clearly going to catch the ball, with the cornerback in no position either to knock the ball away or to intercept. In this case, the cornerback's only option is to deliver one almighty tackle on the receiver at the precise moment he makes contact with the ball, in the hope of preventing a complete reception. In this last resort, the timing of the tackle must be perfect. If the tackle is too early, this and any other form of contact will be ruled as pass interference. If too late, it will succeed only in preventing further gain after the completion.

It is reasonable to assert that man-for-man marking carries an element of risk, in that the defensive back must have lightning reflexes, and a running speed equal to that of the receiver. It was from

Fig 37: *Defensive back competes for ball with wide receiver.*

recognition of this that the more conservative 'zone defense' evolved.

Zone Defense

Before a detailed consideration of the zone defense is made, it is appropriate to consider once more what happens at the snap of the ball. Five receivers could well scatter into the defensive backfield. Of

Fig 38: *Establishing a zone defense. This is only one of several zone systems that are used.*

these five, one will be a primary target, a second will be on standby and the remainder will act as decoys. To defend against this multiple pass offense, the defensive backs and two or three linebackers are allocated areas of authority called zones, shown in Fig 38. The defensive player is responsible for the receiver who enters his zone. The moment the receiver leaves, he becomes the responsibility of someone else. The picture then is one of a distribution of defensive players, holding station amidst the complex pattern running of offensive receivers. Once the pass is on its way, the target is immediately obvious and, at this stage, all defenders converge to the point of reception.

The theory of the zone defense lies in the belief that defenders, declining the challenge of man-for-man marking, will never be beaten badly. Additionally, there will be the opportunity to engage in closer marking during the flight time of the ball, when it is clear just which receiver has been picked out. The weakness, however, lies in the vulnerability of the junction between two zones, since a receiver in this position is as free from close marking as it is possible to be. If the ball can be delivered quickly and accurately to this junction, the chances of a successful completion are high, and with slowly reacting defenders, the opportunity for further progress exists.

The modern squad will be equipped to play both man for man and zone defense, and will change tactics during a game depending on circumstances of scoreline, field position and down status. Consideration of the factors which influence that choice forms part of a later chapter.

There remains a third approach to pass defense, namely the one seeking to defeat the play at source, by tackling the quarterback before he can send the pass on its way, or at the very least, by putting him under great pressure. This is considered next.

The Pass Rush

Consideration of the approaches to pass defense thus far have been made on the assumption that the quarterback will have all the time he needs to deliver the perfect pass. There are occasions in Football when the pass can be predicted with certainty, for example when the offense is losing the game, time is running out, the end zone is far in the distance and it is 3rd down and several yards to go (this would represent a rather miserable situation for the offensive team). In this case, the defense would saturate its territory with pass defenders, willingly giving up rushing yardage and virtually ignoring any attempt to attack the quarterback. However, when a pass is expected and the defense can sense a quarterback's diminishing composure, a defense bristling with confidence will rush the wretched man. This will require the use of a body of defensive players in numbers, greater than can possibly be contained by offensive linemen. Known as 'blitzing', this is not without its risks, for to assemble defenders at the line in readiness for the cavalry charge is to leave the rear sparsely populated and vulnerable should the quarterback do the unthinkable

Fig 39: *Defense in readiness for the blitz. Note that there are now four defensive linemen, two ends and two tackles.*

by getting the pass away. A formation in readiness for the blitz might look something like that in Fig 39.

The list of impositions enforced by a defense with such numerical superiority is impressive. The formation of a pass protection pocket is out of the question. The quarterback, almost certainly under pressure from penetrating defenders, will be forced to shift position, and though he is not yet reduced to scrambling, the possibility of a successful long pass becomes remote. As the pressure of the blitz increases and with distant receivers now obscured by bodies, large and looming larger, the scramble begins and down goes the quarterback.

However, for an offense which correctly anticipates a blitz, there is a way out. To a receiver protected by a blocker or two, a thinly populated rear defense represents easy pickings. Of course, the trick is to release this receiver from the scrimmage area. The offense, expecting the blitz, will go to the line of scrimmage, never intending to contest the physical battle, and disdaining to stem the rush. At the snap of the ball, two offensive linemen, a guard and tackle, will immediately withdraw to re-establish position on one side of the field, roughly parallel to the scrimmage line. A running back, too, will discreetly filter out to this same side. The hope is that to the blitzing throng, blinded by the hunger for quarterback meat, this shift will go

7yds

Fig 40: *Early stage in the screen pass play. The quarterback drops back into passing position. Right guard and right tackle withdraw to right after partial block. Tight end slips past defensive end after partial block. Running back discreetly filters off to right. Wide receiver and flanker run decoy patterns.*

undetected. The quarterback needs only to loop the ball over the heads of the blitzing defenders, to the wide running back who, with the screen of two blockers, will now go to town. This so-called 'screen pass' is the simple and effective counter to the heavy pass rush. Figs 40 and 41 show how the screen pass is executed.

The Personalities

Throughout the first forty years of the NFL, offensive players held the stage while those on defense, whose job was to stifle, spoil and prevent, went largely without public acclaim. Quite properly, the last thirty years have seen some correction of this imbalance. As individuals and in groups, defensive players now pose for the posters.

David 'The Deacon' Jones, defensive end of the Rams, had no peer. Dallas had its 'Doomsday Defense' and Minnesota 'The Purple Gang'. Denver went to Super Bowl XII on the strength of its 'Orange Crush' and Pittsburgh dominated the late 1970s with 'The Steel Curtain'.

Fig 41: *Execution of the screen pass.*

The story continued into the 1980s with the Jets, who developed the 'New York Sack Exchange'. Increasingly, players such as linebacker Lawrence Taylor (Giants) and defensive end Reggie White (Eagles) have been able to dominate the course of a game. In the defensive secondary, too, there have emerged the likes of Ronnie Lott (49ers) and Joey Browner (Vikings), each of whom can have a major impact on the outcome.

CHAPTER V

OFFENSIVE FORMATIONS

So far, the actions of offensive players have been considered on the basis that the offensive team takes up the same standard formation immediately prior to the snap of the ball. To the television viewer, there must appear to be a bewildering variety of formations and, focusing on the quarterback as he does, the cameraman does not make it easy to follow what is going on elsewhere. In reality, a team will use one of a small group of formations. These, together with discussions of their strengths and weaknesses, appear below. The following notation is used in the Figures:

QB	= Quarterback	**FB**	= Fullback
RB	= Running Back	**TB**	= Tailback
WR	= Wide Receiver	**HB**	= Halfback
Fl	= Flanker	**WB**	= Wingback
TE	= Tight End	**C**	= Center
T	= Tackle	**G**	= Guard

The Standard Pro Set

From the pro set (Fig 42), all standard plays are possible and they can be directed to either side. The advantage is that it does not reveal the play to the defense. The flanker stands back from the line of scrimmage, enabling him to be a legal pass receiver. Were he to be on and functioning as the end of the offensive line, the tight end would no longer be eligible to receive a pass. A drawback is that in allowing for itself all the options, there is little opportunity to provide extra weight in support of a particular play. In subsequent formations, provision for the reinforcement of the rush or pass is made.

Fig 42: *The pro set formation.*

The I Formation

In the I formation (Fig 43), the center, quarterback and two running backs stand directly in line with each other. One running back becomes the fullback, the other the tailback. This formation is a slight variation from the pro set and, while still not betraying the intention, gives the tailback an advantage. The fullback is in a better position to act as lead blocker and some tailbacks feel that there is a fraction more time to assess the possibilities at the line of scrimmage.

Fig 43: *The I formation.*

The Power I Formation

As its name implies, the power I formation (Fig 44) is a reinforcement of the I formation, effected by the introduction of another running back (now called a halfback) at the expense of a flanker. From this, a running play is indicated with now both the halfback and fullback able to lead the ball-carrying tailback. With only one receiver wide, the possibility of a long pass is virtually eliminated.

Fig 44: *The power I formation*.

The I Slot

In the I slot formation, the ball-carrying tailback has a lead blocker but, with both the wide receiver and the flanker on the right side, the left side does not present a passing threat.

Fig 45: *The I slot formation*.

The Full House Formation

The full house formation (Fig 46) is clearly designed for a running play. The quarterback can select from three running backs and has a full complement of blockers at the line of scrimmage. With only one wide receiver though, the opportunities for a pass are poor.

Fig 46: *The full house formation.*

Short Yardage Formation

In the short yardage formation (Fig 47), the offense is almost totally committed to the run. It is used therefore only when short yardage is required, either for a touchdown or to gain another 1st down. The ball-carrier will often leap over the pile of linemen rendered prostrate by the mayhem at the line, as is shown in Fig 48.

Fig 47: *The short yardage formation.*

The Twin Set

The twin set, also known as the slot formation (Fig 49), concentrates two pure pass receivers on one side at the expense of neither line blocking nor a running threat. It may well appear to be easing the

Fig 48: *The running back (No 31) takes the air route.*

problems of pass defense and yet, by running their pass patterns in mutual sympathy, the two receivers can cause the opposite effect.

Fig 49: *The twin set (also known as the slot formation).*

The Spread Set

The spread set (Fig 50) is clearly a passing formation with potentially five receivers. The two running backs will stand up at the line of scrimmage and yet far enough away to retain their eligibility as pass receivers.

Fig 50: *The spread set*.

The Shotgun Formation

The shotgun formation (Fig 51) is similar to the spread set but now the tight end is split wider and a running back stands close to the quarterback. The quarterback has greater time to read the actions of defensive players but the requirement for a long snap means that the center is a less effective blocker. The shotgun had been out of favour for 25 years before being revived by Dallas in the late 1970s.

Fig 51: *The shotgun formation*.

Interchange of Formations

It may be part of the offensive strategy to set up the scrimmage using one formation, before changing to another, prior to the snap of the ball. The intention here is to disguise the type and direction of the play. The change may be subtle, for example in the transformation of the I formation to the pro set, as shown in Fig 52.

Fig 52: *Interchange of formation from I formation to pro set.*

Alternatively, the adjustment may be of greater magnitude and strategically more significant as in the transformation of the pro set to the twin set, shown in Fig 53.

For this, while the quarterback is calling signals at the line of scrimmage, the flanker will run laterally 'in motion' to take up his new position. He must not, however, make a move in the offensive direction before the ball is snapped, for this will be penalized and any

Fig 53: *Interchange of formation from pro set to twin set.*

apparent gain resulting from the play will be nullified. The run of the flanker is one of the easiest moves for the new television fan to spot.

The Ace Formation

Known also as 'one-back', 'single-back', 'H-back', 'jayhawk', 'solo' and 'omaha' (it is not an exhaustive list), an essential feature of this formation is that it has just one distinctive running back. Of equal importance, it features another backfield player, often known as the U-back, who will go 'in motion' on almost every play. He may move up to a tight end position or perhaps shift to a wingback spot. As another option he may slot inside the flanker as an extra pure receiver. It is this motion which gives the formation almost limitless versatility and keeps defenses off balance. Alongside the T-formation of Clark Shaughnessy (1940s) and the shotgun formation (early 1950s), the ace formation, which gained popularity in the early 1980s, ranks as one of the great innovations in pro Football history.

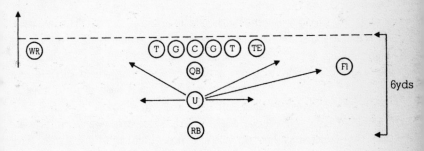

Fig 54: *The Ace formation showing the possibilities for the U-back.*

CHAPTER VI

DEFENSIVE FORMATIONS

Playing good defense is largely a matter of anticipating what the offense will do. This is not always guesswork. In particular, in the final quarter of the game, the combination of scoreline, field position and time remaining will virtually dictate the course of action likely to be chosen by the offense. It is possible to identify several defensive alignments, which for reasons of clarity are illustrated showing players essentially in three lines. However, movement in defense, prior to the snap of the ball, is not restricted as it is for offensive players. Defensive linemen will shift from side to side and linebackers will repeatedly charge forward and withdraw. Cornerbacks may line up nose to nose with wide receivers, and safeties may stand just off the shoulder of the defensive end.

Each of the following formations is best regarded, then, as showing starting positions, for each of which subtle adjustments are made. In the Figures for these formations, the following notations are used:

E = Defensive End
T = Defensive Tackle (Nose Tackle in a three-man line)
LB = Linebacker
CB = Cornerback
S = Safety

4-3-4

The 4-3-4 formation (Fig 55) is one of the two used when it is not possible to anticipate the offensive play. A four-man front will generate an effective pass rush. Three linebackers are sufficient to reinforce the defensive line facing a frontal assault, to provide lateral coverage against the end run and to defend against the short pass over the middle. Four defensive backs are adequate for pass coverage.

Fig 55: *4-3-4 formation*.

3-4-4

The 3-4-4 formation (Fig 56) is the other formation commonly adopted. Indeed, in recent years it has been taken up by the majority of clubs. It is felt that the extra linebacker gives greater effectiveness against the frontal assault, but it is slightly vulnerable against a pass since the weaker pass rush, by only three linemen, allows the quarterback a longer time to select his target.

Pass Defense Formations

When the offense needs a gain of greater than 7 yards on a particular down (usually 3rd down) to maintain the momentum of its

Fig 56: *3–4–4 formation*.

drive, a pass may be safely anticipated. Defensive backs are therefore reinforced at the expense of linebackers. The following formations can be seen as evolving from the 4–3–4 and are varying shades of so-called 'prevent defenses'. The moment play begins, linebackers and safeties will usually set up a patchwork of zones, since this is considered the most effective way of preventing the long pass completion. Cornerbacks may initially play man for man, before withdrawing to join the zone system. The following three formations retain the capability to mount a pass rush.

Fig 57: *4–2–5 formation, also known as the nickel defense.*

4–2–5, the Nickel Defense

In the nickel defense (Fig 57), the defensive backs are reinforced by a safety, at the expense of a linebacker, affording *five* pass defenders. Thus the term 'nickel', which arises through allusion to the coin which has a 5-cent value.

4–1–6, the Dime Defense

In the dime defense (Fig 58), two linebackers are replaced by safeties, and the name 'dime' arises by allusion to the coin of increased value.

Fig 58: *4–1–6 formation, also known as the dime defense.*

3–1–7, the Penny Defense

I have not the remotest idea why such an insignificant coin as the penny should be victimized in description of this most bizarre of formations (Fig 59). Indeed, it should not go unmentioned that the penny defense, an innovation of the 1980s, is designed for use only in the most hair-raising of circumstances.

Fig 59: *3–1–7 formation, also known as the penny defense.*

5–1–5

As an alternative philosophy, to combine a heavy pass rush with a well-stocked backfield, but again at the expense of the linebackers, the defense can choose a 5–1–5 formation (Fig 60).

Fig 60: *5–1–5 formation.*

7–1–3

In defense of what may be inches of ground, say close to the end zone, where the offense will use a short yardage play, a seven-man front line will be used. A frontal offensive assault is most likely, but to counter the surprise pass, three defensive backs are retained in the 7–1–3 formation (Fig 61). Needless to say, all potential receivers will be closely marked once the ball is snapped.

Fig 61: *7–1–3 formation*.

Situational Substitution

The 1980s will be remembered for having been the decade during which defenses began making many substitutions on every down in response to the ever-changing kaleidoscope presented by the offenses. It is now the norm for a formal defensive end to be replaced by a specialist pass rusher, perhaps even on 2nd down and especially when the offense has been restricted to a short gain on 1st down. In many circumstances it makes more sense to redefine a pass-rushing defensive end as an outside linebacker. In San Francisco's so-called 'elephant defense' a strong safety lines up as one of only two linebackers (there are five defensive backs), with a bias to the outside. The Rams' 'nickel defense' represents the ultimate in that, of the starting eleven players, it uses only five.

CHAPTER VII

SPECIAL TEAMS

In circumstances when the ball is going to be kicked, both offense and defense will bring on their 'special teams'. There are four such occasions: at a kickoff, when punting, for a field goal attempt and in converting a touchdown.

THE KICKOFF

The team which wins the toss has a choice of two options: (a) to kick off or receive the kick, or (b) to select which goal to defend. The loser is given the other option. At the beginning of the second half, the team which lost the initial toss now has the choice. It is therefore possible, though unlikely, that a team will kick off at the beginning of each half. More usually, a team will opt for facing the kickoff and the opportunity to start a drive with a four-down series. In addition, to restart the game after a touchdown, with or without successful conversion, and after a successful field goal, the scoring team kicks off. This is another difference from rugby, in which the team which has just scored receives (faces) the kickoff. Figures 62 and 63 show the likely positions of the players at the kickoff.

In the formal circumstances described above, a team kicks the ball, supported by a plastic tee, from its own 35-yard line, and it is immediately of great importance to consider the regulations governing possession. At any point following the kickoff, the receiving team can gather the ball and establish possession.

Fig 62: *Kicking team in readiness for the kickoff.*

However, once the ball has travelled 10 yards, or has been touched by a player of the receiving team, the kicking team can gather the ball and gain possession. Not wanting to present the opposition with good field position which would result from a short kick, the kicking team will thump the ball as far as possible downfield. From this, one of three things can happen.

First, if the ball passes through the end zone (unlikely), the opposition restarts play with a four-down series from its own 20-yard line. Secondly, if an opposition player establishes possession, within his own end zone, but declines any run back, again play restarts at the 20-yard line. Finally, from any point of the field, including the end zone, the opposition player might run the ball back up the field

Fig 63: *Player positions for a kickoff. The defensive players marked D1 are in readiness for short kickoff (unlikely) before dropping back to form blocking pattern together with defensive players marked D2. Either of the kick return specialists marked KR will catch the ball, with the other blocking on the return run.*

until he is grounded. Play then restarts with a four-down series on or inside the hashmarks, corresponding to the point at which the runback was halted.

It is important to re-emphasize that at all times during the kickoff play, the kicking team will compete for possession. Thus, if the kick receiver fails to gather the ball, the kicking team can recover possession. Furthermore if, during the kick return, the ball is fumbled (dropped), either accidentally or as the result of a tackle, it can be recovered by the kicking team, which then becomes the team in possession and on offense.

In normal play, the kick return specialist will catch the ball some 5 yards out from his own end zone, and will immediately begin the return run. Taking care to remain behind the ball until it has been kicked, all 11 players of the kicking team will tear downfield to tackle the runner who, as always in Football, is not alone. His own team will be blocking the opposition, not in a haphazard way but in a collective effort to establish and maintain a corridor, along which he can run freely. In extreme cases, he will go 'all the way' for a touchdown, as did Stanford Jennings of Cincinnati in Super Bowl XXIII. More usually the return run will cover some 20 yards.

For the kicking team, the emphasis will be on downfield pursuit, and the squad will therefore contain several speedy linebackers and defensive backs. The kick return squad, for which the emphasis will be on blocking protection, will consist of mobile blockers. The requirements of a kick returner must closely approach those of a running back but, as it is a tough job, the star runner will never be risked. The responsibility usually falls to the first- or second-year player, still learning his trade and playing second or third fiddle to the established running back pair.

Finally, as a point of law, if the kickoff goes out of bounds over the sideline without having been touched by a player of either team, the receiving team is given the options of taking possession either 30 yards from the spot of the kick, or at the out-of-bounds spot.

PUNTING

There is a world of difference between a kickoff and a punt. First, punting takes place from a down position (a set piece scrimmage), usually on 4th down. Secondly, the specialist punter will have to catch the ball tossed directly backwards (long snap) by the center, before applying the boot. In addition, the opposition will charge the punter in an attempt either to tackle him, or at the very least deflect

Fig 64: *Player positions for the punt. The punt return specialist, marked PR, awaits the punt. The defensive ends, marked DE, will charge the punter. The punt specialist blocker, marked PB, waits to protect the punter if necessary. The punter, marked P, awaits the long snap from center, marked C.*

the ball. A punt is therefore very different from a kickoff which takes place in unhurried circumstances and from a specific field position (35-yard line).

Another difference is that the punting team can send two wide players downfield, *at the moment the ball is snapped*. This means that, even before the ball is punted, there will be two potential tacklers already some 10 yards closer to the specialist punt returner than would be the case from a kickoff. To amplify this advantage, the punter will hoist the ball as high as possible, giving maximum 'hang time'. Once on its way then, the punt is not unlike the Garyowen or 'up an' under' of rugby. Player positions for the punt are shown in Fig 64 and the punter in action in Fig 65.

Fig 65: *The punter in action, protected by two blockers*.

The unfortunate punt returner is in the position of waiting to catch the ball, falling from on high, to the ominous thunder of approaching footsteps. One of three things usually happens. By raising his arm and waving it from side to side, he can signal his intention to make a 'fair catch'. If he can complete the catch, he must not be tackled, but at the same time he is not allowed a return run. Play restarts with a 1st down at the point of the fair catch. As a second option, he can ignore the ball, allowing it to land, bounce and roll harmlessly downfield. He is safe in this since, *if he does not touch the ball*, then neither can the punting team. Play restarts with a 1st down at the point where the ball comes to rest. If this point is in the end zone, play restarts from the 20-yard line. Finally, he can catch the ball and attempt a return run, with the usual blocking support, though now less effective than for a kick return. Again, should he fumble, possession can be re-established by the punting team which then regains offensive status. It is not surprising that a punt return will go for an average of 8.5 yards only.

As a point of law, should the punted ball go over the sideline, play restarts with a 1st down to the receiving team, from the hashmark corresponding to the yardage marker of the point where the ball went out of play. To take advantage of this, the punter will attempt to kick the ball out of play as close as is possible to the opposition goal line, since this would pre-empt any return run. Clearly, this point would be close to the cornerflag, in the region known as 'coffin corner'.

FIELD GOAL ATTEMPT

For a field goal attempt, which is equivalent to a penalty goal or drop goal in rugby, there are three key players: the center, the holder and the kicker, whose positions are shown in Fig 66. The center tosses the ball backwards (long snap) to the holder, in a kneeling position, who places the ball on the ground for the immediate kick. This is

Fig 66: *Player positions for a field goal attempt. The holder, marked H, awaits a long snap from the center, marked C, to place the ball for the kicker, marked K. The defensive ends, marked DE, will charge the kicker around the ends.*

Fig 67: The holder (No 85) holds the ball for the kicker (No 10).

shown in Fig 67. All kicks take place from a set piece scrimmage position. The distance of the kick can be misleading, because the actual kick takes place from a point some 7 yards back from the scrimmage line, and the goal posts are based on the back line of the end zone. Thus a kick originating from a down on the 25-yard line will have to travel 42 yards to clear the crossbar. Should the kick be unsuccessful, play will restart with a 1st down to the opposition on that very same 25-yard line which was the original line of scrimmage.

The defending team will attempt to charge the kicker from around the ends of the line, and also to block the kick with a well-timed leap.

The kicker must therefore achieve early elevation of the ball. This presents a problem for the longer, say 50-yard, kick since, for this, the greater carry requires an initially lower trajectory.

'FAKE' FIELD GOALS AND PUNTS

It should be remembered that, even after setting up to take a punt or field goal attempt, the kicking team may choose to try to gain a 1st down by running or passing the ball, since after all it is still a 4th-down play. Of course, a kicking formation is hardly conducive to rushing or passing success, and yet the element of surprise is in favour of the kicking team. On a 'fake' field goal play, the holder will pretend to place the ball down for the kicker before rolling out, either to run with the ball or pass to a receiver who will have drifted downfield, as surreptitiously as possible. To allow for this possibility, the holder is often a reserve quarterback.

On a 'fake' punt play, the punter makes no bones about it. On receiving the snapped ball, he will run for daylight (and his life) always with the knowledge of just how many yards are needed to gain a 1st down and maintain the momentum of the drive.

The success of 'fake' field goals and punts depends upon surprise, an element which is lost if the tactic is over-used, hence its rarity.

TOUCHDOWN CONVERSION

For a touchdown conversion (extra point attempt), the line of scrimmage is the 2-yard line, and again the crucial feature is the smooth transfer of the ball from the center, via the holder, to the kicker. This achieved, the kick of approximately 20 yards from dead centre is simple. A specialist will miss one or two while kicking 40 in a 16-game season. There is, however, no margin for error, since a bad snap from the center, or a fumble by the holder, gives the kicker no time for recovery. Fig 68 shows the player positions for a touchdown conversion.

END ZONE

2-yd line

9-yd line

Fig 68: *Player formation for a touchdown conversion. The holder, marked H, awaits a long snap from the center, marked C, to place the ball for the kicker, marked K. The defensive ends, marked DE, will charge the kicker around the ends.*

CHAPTER VIII

STRATEGY AND TACTICS

Team strategy is the prerogative of the Head Coach, and while he may well delegate matters of tactical detail to his assistant coaches, he is the general with overall control. He will almost always instruct the quarterback on what the next play should be. He will do this either by using a coded hand signal from the sideline or, exploiting the free substitution rule, he will send on the information with a replacement player.

For much of the NFL's history, virtually every offense used rushing as its cornerstone. However, following the rules changes of the late 1970s, increasingly, teams have opted for a mixture of run and pass to the extent that, sensibly, it is no longer possible to make many general statements. Thus, whereas rushing used to be the standard tactic for establishing momentum, more recently a selection of short passes has been found to be equally effective. Of course there are teams which have a distinct preference for the run or the pass. Sometimes it is a tradition which goes back many years. The Raiders, for example, always have loved to use the long pass. However, most teams will mix their plays. Having said all this, there do remain circumstances under which the likelihood of a particular play is high.

For example, on 3rd down with 6 or more yards to go for a 1st down, a pass is probable. Again, 3rd and 2 from a safe midfield area often signals a long pass. In addition, when the team on offense is losing by a margin greater than 3 points and is some way from its opponents' end zone with time running out, a passing play is almost a certainty. This, though, need not necessarily be a bomb, since the long pass against a defense primed to expect it has a poor chance of success. The wily quarterback will often opt for the short or medium pass down the sideline. Once completed, the receiver can step out of bounds, in this way stopping the clock. The whole play may take up only five seconds of game time, and, by this means, the offense can leapfrog down the field in less than a minute. This is the so-called 'two-minute drill', since it is the last resort, usually reserved for the final two minutes of a half.

Rushing still is regarded as safer than passing, simply because there are fewer things that can go wrong. It means that a team penned deep in its own territory – where an error could be critical – will usually opt to rush. Again, when committed to attempting a field goal, a team will nudge its way into position using rushing plays. This usually happens late in a game when a field goal will decide the outcome. Finally, every team which has a lead, and wishes simply to use up the game clock, is almost certain to use rushing plays.

However, in American Football, nothing is etched in stone. And as with most other team sports, the use of unexpected tactics often brings dramatic success.

One may wonder why there is virtually no lateral passing in American Football, since to string together a series of passes, as in rugby, is quite legal. However, should the ball go astray during transfer from one offensive player to another, bouncing erratically as it would, it could be recovered by players of either team. Curiously, and I am not aware of the philosophical basis for the rule, should the defense recover the ball, it may *not* be advanced as part of that play unless the ball is intercepted. This is to be contrasted with the recovery of a fumbled ball, that is, a ball dropped by a player previously in full control, which *may* be advanced. To this extent, turning over the ball to the opposition during a lateral passing sequence is not quite the catastrophe a fumble would be. Nevertheless, running the risk of relinquishing possession is considered, in itself, sufficient reason to restrict lateral passing only to the most desperate occasions.

For the defense, which is of course aware of the strengths of the opposition, there is always a problem. They may well try to guess the intentions of the offense and against, say, a suspected powerful rush, reinforce the line by all four linebackers taking close order and with a safety up at the line of scrimmage. Yet to do this weakens the defensive backfield and will serve to enhance what may otherwise be a moderate passing threat. On the other hand, a defense can pay closer attention to potential pass receivers, but only at the expense of numbers at the line of scrimmage, thus enhancing the rushing potential of the offense. Under normal circumstances, early in the game and when prediction of the imminent play is impossible, a standard 3-4-4 formation will be adopted. In this, the two central linebackers will be concerned primarily with the frontal assault while the two outside linebackers will play with pass defense in mind.

Occasionally, a team in possession will *deliberately* concede a safety to the opposition. This might happen when the team on offense is in the lead by 6–8 points, late in the game, but is pinned down close to its own end zone. On every punting play, into which the offense is likely to be forced, there is always the chance that the punt can be charged down and even recovered for a touchdown by the team facing the punt. In this case, on 4th down, the quarterback or the punter might deliberately retreat over his own back line to concede a two-point safety. The benefit comes on the ensuing free kick (it can be kicked or punted), which, though from the 20-yard line, can be taken in unhurried circumstances with no possibility of being charged down. Of course, 2 points have been conceded, but the hope is that the opposition will take over possession needing to travel much further for a score than would have been the case following a normal punt.

CHAPTER IX

PENALTIES, TIMING AND THE OFFICIALS

PENALTIES

Penalties are assessed in terms of yardage lost by the offending team. A minor infringement will cost 5 yards while those involving moderate physical contact or significant technical violations cost 10 yards. For an act of horror, usually associated with the possibility of serious injury, 15 yards are charged. In the extreme case of unqualified violence, the player is sent off. The referee does not pussyfoot around; the rules are rigidly enforced and the players do not usually complain. However, unlike the case in most sports, only the individual offender is penalized; he may be replaced legally by another player.

The system is best explained from the starting point of a simple example, with the offensive team at 1st and 10 on its own 30-yard line. Play begins and the result is a 12-yard pass completion, but during this, an official spots an infringement by the *offense*. He does *not* blow a whistle, he does *not* stop play from continuing, but rather he throws down a yellow flag at the point of infringement. The play is allowed to run its full course until the ball is dead and signalled as such by a whistle. The referee then has a discussion with, in this case, the defending team captain, who is given the option to accept or decline the penalty ruling. Obviously, he will accept and the offensive gain will be nullified. If the judgement is a 5-yard penalty, the ball is returned to the original line of scrimmage, and then taken a further 5 yards back. The team on offense retains possession and is now on its own 25-yard line, but more importantly, *it retains the former down*. Play resumes with a 1st and 15 on the 25-yard line.

There will be occasions when it would be to the disadvantage of the defending team to accept the penalty judgement. For example, let us assume again the offense is on its 30-yard line, but now at 4th and 10. Suppose the play was a 7-yard gain, but in the process the offense incurred a 5-yard penalty. If the defending team accepts the judgement, the ball is placed on the 25-yard line and play resumes with a 4th and 15. Yet by accepting the apparent benefit of a 5-yard penalty against the offense, the defense is allowing the offense to replay that 4th down. They are being allowed another opportunity to gain a 1st down, another bite at the cherry. Sensibly, the defending team captain would *decline* the penalty for, since the play had gained only 7 yards, the team on offense would have to transfer possession to the team on defense, in accordance with the four-down/10-yard system.

The same holds true for the team on offense, in the event that the defending team commits a foul. For example at 4th down and 7 yards to go, on its 30-yard line, the offense gains 9 yards on the play, during which the defense is guilty of a foul incurring a 5-yard penalty. Were the offense to accept the judgement, the 9-yard gain would be nullified and they would be required to replay the 4th down which would then be 4th and 2 to go, from the 35-yard line. The 5-yard penalty would be *declined* since, by having gained 9 yards on the play and ignoring the penalty allowance, the offense has earned another series of four downs.

In certain cases, a loss of down is automatic following infringement by the offense, particularly in circumstances associated with passing the ball (discussed in the Rules section). Additionally, for a guilty defense, a yardage penalty might be added on to the gain made by the offense resulting from that play. For example, if during a successful pass play, a defender 'roughs' the passer (discussed in the Rules section), the 15-yard penalty would be added to the yards gained by the successful pass.

The application of advantage preceded by discussion is not

unique to American Football. In rugby, there is choice following infringement at a line-out (throw-in not straight), and for offside after a punt. In soccer too, advantage may be applied, but in this the referee is sole arbiter, and there is no discussion.

TIMING

The game is played in four 15-minute quarters, with a 15-minute break (half time) between the second and third quarters. However, a whole game, including half time, will last in excess of three hours, because when the ball is not in play, the game clock is stopped. This leads to a great deal of stopping and starting, which can initially be an irritation for British fans accustomed to the continuous play of soccer and rugby. Yet it makes sense for two good reasons. First, the fans pay to see an hour of Football, this in itself being sufficient reason for regulating the duration of play. Secondly, it prevents the sordid exhibition of time wasting, which is seen in many games, particularly soccer. So it is of no use to belt the ball into the stands, to feign injury, or to hold onto the ball while taking up position after having conceded a free kick.

Generally the game clock will run while normal play is in progress and the ball remains inbounds. For all those occurrences which would lead to the loss of valuable playing time, the game clock is stopped.

There are two clocks in operation. One is the game clock which indicates the time remaining in the quarter. The other, the 45/30-second clock, is used only to regulate the time between downs. It is perhaps best to illustrate the workings of the timing system by describing a drive downfield (normal play).

In the attempt to speed up the game, without sacrificing the quality of play, in 1988 the NFL replaced what was known as the 30-second clock by the 45/30-second clock. As implied, it can be set to run for either 45 or 30 seconds and it is this clock which governs the time in between plays. Let's imagine a normal drive in which the offense uses a running play. When the play terminates, the 45-second clock is set in motion. It means that the quarterback is allowed 45 seconds to initiate the next play from scrimmage. If he overruns the 45 seconds, he is charged with a delay-of-game penalty. The game clock, meanwhile, has continued to run, but stops with the penalty and restarts on the next snap. Again, if a forward pass is incomplete, the 45/30-second clock is started immediately the play is over. However, by rule, the game clock is stopped and restarts only when the ball is snapped. The 30-second time interval comes into effect only when the official feels that 45 seconds would not give the quarterback a reasonable time to organize his unit for the next play. As an example, such an occasion might be when the officials have to unpile a mountain of bodies in the search for the ball before establishing the new scrimmage spot. Furthermore, 45 seconds might not be a reasonable time interval if a penalty needs to be assessed. In these cases, once the ball has been respotted, the 30-second clock begins to wind down. A more complete list of occasions when the game clock is stopped is given in the Rules section.

Each team is given an opportunity to stop the game clock (take a 'time-out') three times in each half, to allow the quarterback or defensive captain to discuss tactics with his coaches. However, recognizing that, quite often, these time-outs are used simply to stop the game clock, in 1988 the NFL introduced a three-tier system. For all except the final two minutes of a half, a time-out lasts for 90 seconds if the TV company wishes to run a commercial, but lasts only 40 seconds if this is not the case. In the final two minutes of a half, all time-outs last just 40 seconds.

Finally, and one suspects simply to allow for the emotional build-up to the grand finale, the game clock is stopped officially two minutes before the end of each half. It restarts when the ball is snapped to begin the final two minutes of play.

THE OFFICIALS

The standard dress for officials is shown in Fig 69. The referee is the only one who wears a white cap.

The Referee is the senior official and final arbiter in all matters concerning the rules of the game. He concentrates largely on the snap of the ball and the movements of the quarterback and running backs.

Fig 69: An official.

END ZONE

The Umpire observes the actions of offensive interior linemen.

The Head Linesman rules on the movement of players, at the line of scrimmage, immediately prior to the snap of the ball.

The Line Judge has similar responsibilities to those of the Head Linesman, but in addition he will observe the actions of receivers close to the line of scrimmage.

The Back Judge rules on matters concerning pass receptions, including any interference and the inbounds completion of a pass.

The Side Judge operates essentially as does the Back Judge, but in addition looks for illegalities in line play.

The Field Judge observes plays associated with the tight end.

Of course, all the officials have complete mastery of the rules, and can be consulted on those occasions when the official normally responsible for spotting infringements is unsighted. The positions which they adopt immediately prior to the snap of the ball, are shown in Fig 70.

The Eighth Official

Beginning in the 1986 season, after discussions going back some years, the NFL began using TV instant replay to aid the officials on the field. Subsequently, in the 1988 season, the adjudicator in the TV booth became the eighth official.

He views every play as it happens on television and decides whether or not the play needs any further consideration. If, in his opinion, he feels that the play should be reviewed, the umpire on the field is contacted immediately. If not, there is no interruption of the normal flow of play.

The replay official watches replay(s) on one or both of his monitors and, when satisfied, informs the umpire of his decision. The referee makes the announcement to the crowd in the normal way.

The use of instant replay is limited to plays of possession or touching, for example, fumbles, receptions, interceptions and muffs. In

Fig 70: *The positions
of the officials prior
to the snap of the ball.*

addition, it is used on plays governed by the sidelines, end lines, plane of the end zone and line of scrimmage.

It is important to note that there remain many aspects of rules enforcement in which instant replay is not used, for example, all acts of illegal contact such as pass interference, holding, illegal use of the hands and grasping the facemask.

CHAPTER X

OFFICIAL SIGNALS AND RULES

TOUCHDOWN (6 pts), EXTRA POINT (1 pt), FIELD GOAL (3 pts)

A **touchdown** is normally scored by rushing or passing but there are other ways worth bearing in mind, as follows:

(a) Following a fumble recovery by the offense (except on 4th down) or the defense, or an interception by a defensive player, the ball can be advanced as part of that play. Note that in the final two minutes of a half, of all the offensive players, only the player who fumbled may recover and advance.

(b) On establishing possession following recovery of a blocked field goal attempt or punt (for the offense, only behind the line of scrimmage in both cases) the ball can be advanced.

(c) By the direct return of a kickoff or punt.

The **extra point** normally is scored by a kick from a scrimmage on the 2-yard line. However, it is legal both to *run* with the ball or *pass* the ball into the end zone, as for scoring a touchdown. In all cases, though, only one point is scored.

A **field goal** attempt can be made on any down, from any part of the field. If unsuccessful, possession is transferred to the opposition at the previous spot. If that spot was inside the opponents' 20-yard line, play restarts at the 20-yard line. This is known as a **touchback**.

SAFETY (2 pts conceded to the opposition)

A player, in possession of the ball, is trapped within his own end zone or is forced to run out of his own end zone in any direction other than the forward direction. It applies only when the player in possession has entered the end zone under his own impetus. In other words, he has entered his end zone either by choice or obligation, but under his own steam. When a player in possession is tackled in the end zone under the following circumstances, a safety is not conceded but, rather, play restarts with a 1st down on the 20-yard line.

(a)   A player *already in the end zone* gathers a punt, a kickoff or makes either an interception or a fumble recovery.

(b)   A player gathers the ball, say, inter- cepts a pass, and falls into the end zone as part of that action.

FIRST DOWN

From four or fewer downs, 10 or more yards have been gained, thus earning for the offense another series of four downs. As an interesting note for statisticians, on all rushing and passing touchdowns, the offensive team is credited with a 1st down.

LOSS OF DOWN

This signal indicates a loss of down associated with a penalty.

DEAD BALL OR NEUTRAL ZONE ESTABLISHED

This signals that the ball is dead and that the next down can begin at any time. 4th down is indicated when the referee clenches the fist of his raised hand.

TIME-OUT

An official on the field, or the official clock operator, will stop the game clock under the following circumstances:

(a) At the request for a team time-out by a player of either team. Three team time-outs are allowed in each half. Except for the final two minutes of a half, a team time-out is 90 seconds unless the TV company does not wish to run a commercial, in which case the time-out lasts 40 seconds. Inside the final two minutes of a half, a team time-out is 40 seconds.

(b) Two minutes before the end of a half.

(c) Following a score.

(d) Following an infringement of the rules. Note that, inside the final two minutes of a half, a team can not stop the game clock by deliberately infringing the laws. In this case, after the penalty has been assessed, ten seconds are run off the game clock, which is then re-started immediately.

(e) Following a change in possession.

(f) When a fair catch is made.

(g) When a forward pass is incomplete.

(h) When a player is injured.

(i) When the ball goes over the sideline.

(j) When necessary to unpile the players in order to spot the ball.

Two important consequences of the rules governing timing are listed below:

(a) A team in the lead and close to the end

of normal time will attempt to keep the clock running by using only rushing plays, particularly staying inbounds. This is known as 'ball control'.

(b)   A team losing and with little time remaining is likely to attempt passes directed towards the sidelines on most downs. Having made the reception, the receiver will step over the sideline, thus stopping the clock. Even should the pass be incomplete, the clock will be stopped. This tactic, often used either inside or close to the final two minutes of a half, is known as the 'two-minute drill'.

TIME-IN or RESTART THE GAME CLOCK WHEN THE WHISTLE BLOWS

This indicates that the game clock must continue to run after the following events which may lead to doubt for the clock operator:

(a)   When a play has come to an end, close to the sideline but still inbounds.

(b)   Where necessary after a brief pause to allow for spotting the ball.

PENALTY REFUSED, INCOMPLETE PASS, PLAY OVER, MISSED KICK AT GOAL

Penalty Refused: There are occasions when it would be to the disadvantage of a team to enforce a penalty incurred by the opposition. For example, the offense would decline any penalty following an infringement by the defense if, on that play, the offense had scored a touchdown or made a gain which, by acceptance of the ruling, would be nullified.

Incomplete Pass: A forward pass is dropped or goes out of bounds.

Play Over: Play on a particular down is over.

Missed Kick at Goal: A field goal or extra point attempt is unsuccessful.

DELAY OF GAME

This usually arises when the quarterback overruns the 45/30-second clock and, more rarely, when a player, either offensive or defensive, behaves in a manner designed to prevent play from continuing normally. In each case the penalty is the loss of 5 yards with retention of down. For example, at 2nd and 10 on the offense's 30-yard line, if the quarterback overruns the 45/30-second clock, plays restarts with a 2nd and 15 on the offense's 25-yard line.

Should a team not be ready to play at the beginning of a half (this is very rare), the penalty, incurring both the loss of the coin toss option *and* the loss of 15 yards, is severe.

ILLEGAL MOTION

One offensive player – in the backfield – may be 'in motion', running laterally or in a direction back and away from the line of scrimmage during the starting count. However, he must not turn upfield before the ball is snapped. The penalty is a loss of 5 yards but retention of down.

Following a legal shift, all 11 players must remain stationary for at least one second before the ball is snapped. There are no exceptions to this rule.

OFFSIDE or ENCROACHMENT

Offside: This penalty occurs immediately prior to or simultaneous with the snap. Essentially, players of either team may not be in the neutral zone at the moment the ball is snapped.

Encroachment: Defensive players may enter the neutral zone but they must withdraw before the ball is snapped, otherwise they are offside. If a defensive player crosses the neutral zone and makes contact with an offensive player, this is encroachment.

In both cases the penalty is a loss of 5 yards with retention of down.

FALSE START, ILLEGAL FORMATION, ILLEGAL SHIFT

False Start: Once an offensive player has assumed a three-point stance he may not move in any way which might fool a defensive player into thinking that the play has started. Usually, an offensive lineman might prematurely lunge forward.

Illegal Formation: A team is not allowed fewer than seven men on the line of scrimmage (this can include wide receivers and tight ends).

Illegal Shift: After having assumed a set position, two or more players on the offense may legally *shift* to a new stance. However, just one lineman moving after assuming a set position is an illegal shift.

In all three cases the penalty is a loss of 5 yards with retention of down.

ILLEGAL FORWARD PASS

Only one forward pass is allowed. It must be from a scrimmage play, and it must be from behind the line of scrimmage.

(a)   For a forward pass from other than a scrimmage play – say on a punt or kickoff return – the penalty is a loss of 5 yards from the spot of the pass.

(b)   For a second forward pass from behind the line, or for a pass from behind the line of scrimmage after the ball has been across the line of scrimmage, the penalty is the loss of down.

(c)   For a forward pass from beyond the line of scrimmage, the penalty is a loss of down and a loss of 5 yards from the spot of the pass.

INTENTIONAL GROUNDING

At any time a passer may deliberately throw the ball to ground. This he might do when wishing to stop the game clock. However, he is not allowed to throw the ball to ground in the effort to avoid a loss of yardage, for example, when he is in imminent danger of being sacked. The penalty is either the loss of 10 yards and a loss of down, or, if the pass was from more than 10 yards behind the line of scrimmage, a loss of down from that spot. If the spot of the illegal pass was inside the end zone, a safety score is conceded.

PASS JUGGLED INBOUNDS, CAUGHT OUT OF BOUNDS

This concerns the validity of a pass reception. In order to be a legal completion, the receiver must have complete control of the ball and, if in isolation, he must land with both feet inbounds. However, the pass reception would be legal were he to have full control of the ball in the air and yet be driven out of bounds by the force of a tackle, before being able to touch down with his feet.

INELIGIBLE RECEIVER TOUCHES A FORWARD PASS

A forward pass caught or even touched by any offensive player other than an eligible receiver is illegal. The penalty depends on the field location where the ball is touched.

On or behind the line: The penalty is the loss of down at the previous spot. 2nd and 10 from the offense's 30-yard line would become 3rd and 10 from the same spot.

Beyond the line: The penalty is a loss of down at the previous spot *or* a loss of 10 yards with retention of down. In the second alternative, 2nd and 10 on the offense's 30-yard line would become 2nd and 20 on the offense's 20-yard line.

INELIGIBLE RECEIVER DOWNFIELD

This violation is concerned with both passing and punts.

Passing: On passing plays, ineligible receivers are not allowed to travel more than 1 yard beyond the line of scrimmage until the ball has left the passer's hand. Strictly speaking, this violation is one form of pass interference, and it is perhaps for this reason that, in assessing the penalty, the rules makers would appear to be strangely severe on what might appear to be a trivial matter. The penalty is a loss of 10 yards with retention of down.

Punts: On punts, only the two ends are allowed to travel beyond the line of scrimmage, after the ball has been snapped but before it is punted. The penalty is a loss of 5 yards from the previous spot with retention of down.

PASS INTERFERENCE

In recent years, the rules makers have become slightly less severe on defensive players in defining pass interference. For offensive players, the rule begins with the snap of the ball, while for the defense, it begins when the ball is passed. Quite simply, no player of either team may interfere with the attempt of an opposing player to catch a forward pass. When there is no sensible possibility that the ball could have been caught, there is no pass interference. For a guilty offense, the penalty is the loss of 10 yards with retention of down. If the defense is guilty, the offensive team is awarded a 1st down at the point of interference. If this is inside the defensive team's end zone, the 1st down is at the defense's 1-yard line. As a supplementary rule, should there be a personal foul by the defense on the play, any such penalty is added on and assessed from the spot of the foul.

INVALID FAIR CATCH SIGNAL

To signal his intention to make a *fair catch*, when facing a punt or a kickoff, the player raises his arm in the air and waves it from side to side. In violation, typically, the player might forget to wave his arm. The penalty is a loss of 5 yards. Thus, following an invalid fair catch signal on the receiving team's 25-yard line, play resumes with a 1st and 10 on the receiving team's 20-yard line.

ILLEGAL USE OF HANDS, ARMS OR BODY

This rule is primarily concerned with blocking. It is illegal for a player, other than the ball-carrier, to push off an opponent by using his hands or arms during a block. Also, he may not throw his body against a teammate in order to help that player to assist the ball-carrier. The penalty is a loss of 10 yards with retention of down.

HOLDING

It is illegal for an offensive player to grasp hold of an opponent in any way in his attempt to protect the ball-carrier. The penalty for *offensive holding* is a loss of 10 yards with retention of down. A defender is allowed greater use of his hands, particularly when protecting himself and in grappling with a blocking opponent. However, he may not hold onto an opponent in the attempt to protect that player from blocking for the ball-carrier or taking up a position to receive a pass. In the case of *defensive holding* the penalty is a loss of 5 yards and an automatic 1st down to the offense.

TRIPPING

It is illegal to trip an opponent – using the leg, foot, hand or arm – or to obstruct an opponent by contact below the knee, except when that opponent is the ball-carrier, in which case use of the hands and arms is permissible. For *offensive* tripping, the penalty is a loss of 10 yards with retention of down. After tripping by the *defense*, the penalty is a loss of 10 yards and an automatic 1st down to the offense.

CRAWLING, INTERLOCKING INTERFERENCE, PUSHING OR HELPING THE RUNNER

Crawling: This is the attempt by a runner to advance with the ball after he has legally been brought to a halt. The penalty is the loss of 5 yards from the spot where he was originally stopped, with retention of down.

Interlocking Interference: In assisting the runner, blockers may not interlock their arms to form a protective wall. The penalty is the loss of 10 yards with retention of down.

Pushing or helping the runner: In assisting the ball-carrier, a teammate is not allowed to lift him or push him. The penalty is the loss of 10 yards with retention of down.

BALL ILLEGALLY KICKED OR BATTED

Kicking: Unlike in rugby, the ball may not be fly-kicked as a normal part of play.

Batting: A loose ball may not be batted by any player towards an opponent's end zone. This is to be distinguished from actions by any player preventing an opponent from catching a pass.

For both *illegal kicking* and *batting* the penalty is the loss of 10 yards. For a guilty offense, the down is retained while for a guilty defense, the offense, in addition, is awarded an automatic 1st down.

ILLEGAL CONTACT

This is associated with defensive actions against an eligible pass receiver. Within a 5-yard zone downfield from the line of scrimmage, a defender may make and maintain contact with an eligible receiver, though not in violation of the rules governing holding. Beyond the 5-yard zone, the defender may not contact, or bump the receiver in the effort to delay or deflect his downfield movements. The penalty is a loss of 10 yards and an automatic 1st down to the offense.

ILLEGAL BLOCKING BELOW THE WAIST

On kickoff returns, punt returns and during all continuing action following a change of possession – for example, interceptions and fumble recoveries – it is illegal to block below the waist. This is a personal foul, penalized by the loss of 15 yards. Following an illegal block by the return team, the penalty is assessed from the point where possession was first established, *or* from the spot where the illegal block occurred – to the advantage of the opponent.

ILLEGAL CRACKBACK BLOCK

Clipping in close-line play by offensive linemen is legal. However, no player who lines up more than 2 yards outside the tackle, or who lines up in the backfield before taking up a position 2 or more yards outside the tackle, may clip. In addition, if the player is moving towards the ball in a blocking attempt, he may not block below the waist. The penalty is the loss of 15 yards with retention of down.

PERSONAL FOUL

The actions listed under the heading of personal foul are treated with great severity. The penalty is the loss of 15 yards and, in the case of a guilty defense, an automatic 1st down to the offense. Typical infringements include the following:

Striking, kicking and kneeing: These are straight physical assault.

Grasping the facemask: This is a particularly dangerous act, though the rules allow for so-called *incidental* grasping, an act which is penalized by a loss of 5 yards.

Roughing the kicker or passer: This is unnecessary contact after the ball has been kicked or passed.

Piling on: A host of defensive players might descend on the ball-carrier after he has been downed.

Clipping: This is a block from behind and below the waist. It can result in serious knee and lower leg injuries for the player clipped.

Interestingly, over the years since the initial publication of *Guide*, the frequency of the personal foul appears to have declined.

UNSPORTSMANLIKE CONDUCT

This is equivalent to what we in the UK would understand as 'ungentlemanly conduct' and

essentially covers all acts which conflict with the spirit of the game. Such violations might include the use of foul language and taunting an opponent. For an infringement by the offense, the penalty is the loss of 15 yards with retention of down. For a guilty defense, the penalty is the loss of 15 yards and an automatic 1st down to the offense. Prolonged and unseemly celebration by players of either team is treated less severely, with the loss of only 5 yards (no automatic 1st down in this case).

PLAYER DISQUALIFIED

For acts of unqualified violence or complete disregard for authority, the player is sent off the field and may not return. Interestingly, though, he can be replaced by another player in the normal manner of substitution. In that sense, his team is not punished as severely as would be the case in soccer and both codes of rugby.

CHAPTER XI

FOOTBALL TERMINOLOGY

Audible: The signals called out by the quarterback when, at the line of scrimmage, he needs to alter the type of play.

Blitz: A defensive play designed to tackle the quarterback before he can deliver the pass. Usually, linebackers and a safety join in the pass rush. It is a risky play since it exposes the weakened backfield to the passing play if the quarterback can evade the blitz.

Blocking: Deliberately and legally obstructing an opposing player. The blocker is restricted as follows:

(a) he is not allowed to use hands to grab or hold,

(b) he is not allowed to use arms to encircle or trip,

(c) the block must be from a frontal direction.

Blocking is to be distinguished from tackling (allowed only on the man with the ball) for which the only restrictions are those associated with the risk of serious injury, e.g. grabbing an opponent's facemask.

Bomb: A long, spectacular pass.

Bootleg: A surprise run by the quarterback, who will often try to conceal the ball by holding it close to his hip as he runs.

Chain crew: The officials, on the sidelines, who operate a 10-yard measuring chain. If there is a dispute over the yardage gained, the 10-yard chain is brought on and becomes the official measure of the yardage.

Clipping: A form of blocking by contacting an opponent from the rear and below the waist. It is an illegal act unless the action takes place as part of the defensive-offensive line interaction.

Completion: To catch a forward pass.

Cut: A sidestep when running at speed.

Delay of game: The quarterback fails to initiate play within the allowed 45/30 seconds.

Direct snap: The center tosses the ball to a backfield player some way off the line of scrimmage, e.g.

(a) the quarterback in the shotgun formation,

(b) the holder for a touchdown conversion or field goal attempt,

(c) the punter.

Dogging: A pressure play on the quarterback involving linebackers only.

Encroachment: Making contact with an opposing player before the ball is snapped. This usually means that a lineman has wrongly anticipated the snap of the ball and has lunged forward.

Fake: A quarterback pretends to do something in order to confuse the defense. He will 'fake' the handoff to a running back before passing to a receiver.

Flag on the play: The official throws down a yellow handkerchief during play to indicate that an offence has taken place.

Flea-flicker: This is a general term for trick plays involving passing the football. Typically, a quarterback might hand the ball to a running back before withdrawing to a deeper backfield position. The running back then tosses the ball to the quarterback, who throws a forward pass. The idea is that the defensive secondary will be fooled into moving up to defend against a rushing play, leaving deep receivers wide open to catch a pass.

Fumble: The ball is dropped by a player who previously had full control. This can be accidental or as the result of a tackle.

Goal line: The chalk line which marks the beginning of the end zone and separates it from the field of play.

Handoff: The smooth transfer of the ball by the quarterback, usually to a running back.

Hang time: The flight time of a punted ball.

Hashmarks: The lines marking the central strip of playing area, and stretching the length of the field. All formal plays begin within or on the edge of this strip.

Huddle: The grouping of offensive players, having the next play explained, usually by the quarterback.

Incompletion: A forward pass that is not caught within bounds.

Ineligible receiver: The offensive player, usually a lineman, who is not allowed to catch a forward pass.

Ineligible receiver downfield: The ineligible receiver who has moved more than 1 yard beyond the line of scrimmage on a passing play, before the ball is passed.

In motion: An offensive player who, before the snap of the ball, moves to another starting position is said to be in motion. He must run laterally, and is allowed to change direction and turn upfield only after the snap.

Intentional grounding: A pass deliberately thrown to ground by the quarterback, to avoid being tackled in possession for a loss of yards.

Interference block: The travelling block by a player leading the ball-carrier.

Interior lineman: The five players, tackles, guards and center, who form the interior of the offensive line.

Knuckle ball: This is a term borrowed from baseball and used to describe the motion of the ball in flight. Instead of gently rotating about its axis, it tumbles.

Lateral pass: The pass in a sideways or backward direction (as in rugby).

Line drive: A term borrowed from baseball and used to describe a ball which is kicked with great force and which travels a distance, essentially parallel with the ground.

Lineman: A player who forms part of the front line, either offensive or defensive, at the start of a down.

Line of scrimmage: The line (plane) passing through the end of the ball nearest a team's own goal line.

Measuring chain: The official measure of yardage gained. See also under Chain Crew.

Neutral zone: The 11-inch strip of ground, the length of the football, stretching laterally from sideline to sideline and spanning the lines of scrimmage.

Offensive holding: The illegal use of hands by an offensive player in grabbing or holding an opponent.

Offside: A lineman, either offensive or defensive, beyond the line of scrimmage when the ball is snapped, is offside.

Onside kick: The short kickoff, as the alternative to the more usual long kickoff, following a score, used when the kicking team desperately needs to regain possession to score again.

Pass interference: Illegal contact made by either player in the attempt to catch or intercept a forward pass.

Penalty marker: The yellow flag (handkerchief) thrown by an official, while play is in progress, to indicate that an offence has taken place.

Personal foul: An act of violent contact outside the rules of the game, e.g. clipping, late tackle, kicking or punching.

Piling on: The unnecessary adding of players' weight to the tackles of others, once the ball-carrier is clearly downed.

Pitchout: As an alternative to the handoff, when the quarterback tosses the ball laterally to a running back.

Play action: The motion of a quarterback, faking a handoff as a prelude to delivering his pass. As an alternative, he might stand firm in the pass protection pocket.

Pocket: The protected area from inside which the quarterback delivers his pass.

Prevent defense: The deliberate reinforcement of the defensive back-field to amplify the defense against the expected long pass but conceding rushing yardage.

Punt return: The distance of the runback following a successful reception of the punted ball.

Roughing the kicker: The deliberate, forceful and illegal contact with the kicker after he has kicked the ball away.

Roughing the passer: Similar to roughing the kicker, but in this case the illegal contact is with the passer after he has delivered his pass.

Rushing play: Running with the ball following a handoff, pitchout or lateral pass.

Sack: To tackle the quarterback in possession of the ball behind the line of scrimmage.

Shift: The concerted movement of offensive players in adjusting to a new alignment immediately prior to the snap of the ball.

Sideline: Similar to the touchline of soccer and rugby. As in the case of rugby, but not soccer, the sideline is out of bounds.

Snap: The transfer of the ball from the center to the quarterback initiating play at the line of scrimmage. The center, standing with his legs astride, passes the ball back through his legs.

Spearing: The act of diving at a player, helmet first, when he is already clearly grounded.

Stunting: The act of a defensive player who loops round a teammate to penetrate the offensive line through its middle.

Tackling: The act of bringing down or clearly holding with one's arms the man with the ball. See under 'blocking' for the difference between tackling and blocking.

Time-in: The game clock is running.

Time-out: The game clock is stopped either at the request of a player or as directed by the officials.

Touchback: The act of restarting play from the 20-yard line when, following a kick or punt, the ball has passed through the end zone or, having gathered the ball within the end zone, a defender declines any return run.

Two-minute warning: The automatic time-out which occurs two minutes before the end of each half.

Unsportsmanlike conduct: Ungentlemanly conduct.

Yardage: A distance measured in yards.

TIPS FOR TELEVISION VIEWERS

Now that you've read this book, and know what the game is about, you might find the following tips helpful when watching television.

Watch the quarterback As a start, rather than searching for the ball, focus on the quarterback, watching his movements. If he drops straight back he is going to pass, but if he rolls and fakes, you cannot be sure what he will do. Having got used to the fact that he will be floating around in the backfield, the man with all the options, you can start to take in the wider picture of things.

Watch the offensive linemen On a pass play they are not allowed to smash down the field, so very rapidly they will all drop back to form a pocket for the quarterback, confirming the pass. If they all lunge forward, they are clearing the way for a running back.

Watch the man in motion Some teams use a man in motion on many plays and, though he sometimes acts as a decoy, he usually plays a more active part, whether it be turning upfield to receive a pass or throwing a key block.

Identify linebackers and safeties; are they coming or going? Defensive linemen will be bent over with one or both hands touching the ground. Linebackers and safeties will be crouched and hovering. If they rush forward, they are 'blitzing', i.e. trying to nail the quarterback. If they withdraw from the line action, they are almost certainly setting up a zone defensive pattern. There will always be one linebacker, the real killer, who will go for the ball whatever and whoever is in the way.

127

Punting and field goal attempts It is often more fun to watch the defensive players who will charge round the end of the offensive line, trying to block the kick.

Kickoff and punt receiving Anticipating the return run, it is best to focus in front of the punt/kickoff receiver, looking for lead blockers who are trying to establish a running lane to spring him into open field. Once there, he is going 'all the way'.

Time-out Keep a count of these (each team is allowed three in each half) because they are crucial when teams want to stop the clock towards the end of each half.

Try to predict the next play On 3rd down with more than 5 yards to go, a pass is almost certain. This will be strongly indicated if three wide receivers appear in the lineup. When only a short gain is needed, extra offensive linemen, more than seven on the line of scrimmage, will signal a running play.

Sneaky play section

(a) A quarterback will drop back as if to pass but instead will hand the ball to a running back. This is the 'draw' play.

(b) The quarterback might toss the ball to a running back who then throws a forward pass. This is the 'half back option play' and is perfectly legal.

(c) Look for a short kickoff, the 'onside kick', near the end of a half.

(d) Punters, holders and kickers are perfectly entitled to run and pass just as for a formal down.

Illustration Acknowledgement. The publishers wish to thank Michael Hodson Designs for creating the diagrams, and Gerry Malone for the illustrations which appear in this book.